DOSTOEVSKY

CRIME AND PUNISHMENT

NOTES

COLES EDITORIAL BOARD

Bound to stay open

Publisher's Note

Otabind (Ota-bind). This book has been bound using the patented Otabind process. You can open this book at any page, gently run your finger down the spine, and the pages will lie flat.

ABOUT COLES NOTES

COLES NOTES have been an indispensible aid to students on five continents since 1948.

COLES NOTES are available for a wide range of individual literary works. Clear, concise explanations and insights are provided along with interesting interpretations and evaluations.

Proper use of COLES NOTES will allow the student to pay greater attention to lectures and spend less time taking notes. This will result in a broader understanding of the work being studied and will free the student for increased participation in discussions.

COLES NOTES are an invaluable aid for review and exam preparation as well as an invitation to explore different interpretive paths.

COLES NOTES are written by experts in their fields. It should be noted that any literary judgement expressed herein is just that — the judgement of one school of thought. Interpretations that diverge from, or totally disagree with any criticism may be equally valid.

COLES NOTES are designed to supplement the text and are not intended as a substitute for reading the text itself. Use of the NOTES will serve not only to clarify the work being studied, but should enhance the reader's enjoyment of the topic.

ISBN 0-7740-3693-1

© COPYRIGHT 1993 AND PUBLISHED BY
COLES PUBLISHING COMPANY
TORONTO—CANADA
PRINTED IN CANADA

Manufactured by Webcom Limited
Cover finish: Webcom's Exclusive **Duracoat**

CONTENTS

Dostoevsky: Life and Works

Fyodor Mikhailovich Dostoevsky was born in 1821 in Moscow, where his father, a nobleman who had lost his fortune, was resident doctor at a charity hospital. Living on the hospital grounds, young Fyodor acquired an early acquaintance with illness, poverty, and misery which was to serve him well in his later writings. His old-fashioned father saw to it that his children had a strict, authoritarian, and deeply religious upbringing. Fyodor's mother died when he was sixteen, and two years later his father was murdered by his own serfs. Although no one ever learned the full truth about the crime, it was generally believed to be an act of reprisal against the doctor's brutality and severity. Fyodor was deeply shocked by the murder of his father, with whom he had experienced that complex love-hate relationship that occurs in so many of his novels, and he probably never completely recovered from it.

Of the seven Dostoevsky children, Fyodor was closest to his brother, Mikhail, who, from the available evidence, seems never to have fully returned Fyodor's devotion. Fyodor was educated at home until his mother's death, when he was sent to a military engineering school at St. Petersburg. There he was bored and unhappy, but managed to do a great deal of reading, much of it in the works of the German romantic writers. By the time he graduated, four years later, he had decided that he would make literature his career.

His first novel, *Poor Folk,* met with modest success upon its publication in 1846, and Dostoevsky was hailed by the noted critic, Belinsky, as a great new talent. He continued writing and became a member of a liberal group called the Petrashevsky Circle, which met to discuss politics and literature. In 1849, all the members of this group were arrested as subversives by a government which was at that time extremely reactionary and totalitarian. They were sentenced to die before a firing squad for allegedly plotting against the regime. It was a cruel trick, for as they were about to be executed the prisoners were informed that their lives had been spared and their sentences commuted to hard labor. One man went mad from the strain and shock. All his life Dostoevsky remembered the feelings of the man condemned to death, and used this knowledge repeatedly in his later works. He served his term of four years at hard labor in Siberia among thieves and murderers but, incredibly, he was not embittered by what he suffered there. His only reading matter was the Bible, and he meditated deeply on the Gospels and the idea of salvation through suffering. He rejected his youthful liberalism for an antirationalist faith and a belief in the sacred destiny of the Russian masses, of those wretched souls who shared his life for four miserable years. He came to feel that it was through these criminals, most of them deeply conscious of their sinfulness and humbly dependent on the mercy of God, that he was enabled to find his new faith. It is probable, too, that a deeply ingrained sense of sin and guilt was part of his character. Many critics have suggested that he felt in some obscure way responsible for the death of his father, and that this accounts for the theme of parricide in his works. Thus, he may have believed his sufferings were deserved.

After these agonizing years, he was sent as a private to military service at an isolated Asian outpost, and remained there for another five years. When he was finally permitted to return to St. Petersburg he was thirty-eight and had acquired a wife, a sickly woman who had a mentally retarded son. It was not a happy marriage, and Dostoevsky spent much time travelling abroad alone.

During the twenty-three years between his return to St. Petersburg and his death, he worked furiously as a journalist, editor, and novelist. He still endured much unhappiness: he had suffered from fits of epilepsy since his imprisonment; his wife died and he supported her son; during his travels in Europe he lost much money through gambling and had an unhappy love affair with a young woman writer, Polina Suslova; he lost his beloved brother, Mikhail, and undertook the support of his widow and children. His most important works were written during this period: *Notes from Underground* in 1864, *Crime and Punishment* in 1866, *The Idiot* in 1868, *The Possessed* in 1871, and *The Brothers Karamazov* in 1880. In 1867, he married his stenographer, a young, energetic, and devoted woman who was his major comfort in the later years of his life. His financial difficulties continued, but after the success of *The Possessed,* Dostoevsky's wife began to manage his business affairs and their circumstances improved. Despite the death of two of their four children, Dostoevsky's final years were on the whole fruitful and happy. His future plans included a Russian *Candide,* a book about Christ, and an epic which he tentatively entitled *The Life of a Great Sinner,* but he died less than three months after finishing *The Brothers Karamazov,* which was to have been the first part of this vast work.

Historical Background

The iron regime of Czar Nicholas I began with the Decembrist Revolt of 1825. This first attempt at reform in an absolute despotism ended in catastrophe. Nicholas had the leaders hanged and scores of the nobility and intelligentsia exiled to Siberia. The Czar emerged as a complete monster. Public opinion was stifled, strict censorship laws were strictly enforced, and a secret police spy system made even the most harmless kind of political activity extremely dangerous. This was the Czar who condemned Dostoevsky to be shot for his activities in the Petrashevsky Circle, allowing all the preparations for the execution to proceed through to the eleventh hour.

In 1855, Alexander II came to the throne. Russia experienced a period of relative liberalism during his reign, which lasted until his assassination in 1881, the year of Dostoevsky's death. This was the period of the "Great Reforms": the emancipation of the serfs in 1861; the granting of the first real local self-government; judicial reform that saw the introduction of the jury system; and a military reform that created a democratic universal military service. All these had a profound effect on Russian life.

Despite Alexander II's enlightened policy, revolutionary movements and opposition of all kinds continued to grow. Criticism of the government was common among all classes. The nobility wanted to share in the governing power as a compensation for its lost social and economic privileges. The new social class, the intelligentsia, rapidly forming from among children of the clergy, civil servants, and the impoverished nobility, was the most radical, demanding rapid political changes and social revolution. More moderate criticism appeared in the legalized press, the more bitter criticism in the revolutionary works published abroad.

Antigovernment activity increased in the 1870's, and desire for a parliament to complete the unfinished reforms grew. After the Turkish War of 1877-78 and Bulgaria's new constitution, the desire for a Russian constitution became strong. Revolutionary activity was constantly increasing. The intellectuals began a movement "to the people," an attempt to arouse the masses. The government grew uneasy and began to use more repressive measures. Around 1875, the revolutionaries turned to the use of terrorism and assassination. From 1879 on, the Czar himself was the object of these attempts at assassination, and one was finally successful in 1881.

Slavophilism and Pan-Slavism

Slavophilism and Pan-Slavism, two related movements with which Dostoevsky identified himself, were essentially outgrowths of an attempt, dating back to the seventeenth century and earlier, to improve the Slavic self-image. Slavs need not cringe before foreigners, they are not by nature inferior, the argument went. Russia's boorishness was simply a manifestation of its youth as a nation.

The Slavophiles of the nineteenth century, while sharing with the Westerners the belief that reform in the existing structure was necessary, denounced imitation of the West. They felt that there was no need for Russia to follow the road already travelled by Europe, which in Dostoevsky's mind was a vast cemetery where beneath marble monuments slept the spirits of the departed great. They were convinced that somewhere in Russia's past must be an ideal principle which, when nurtured, would put Russia in the forefront of world development. They believed, moreover, that Russia had a messianic role to play in

3

the world. Her mission was to carry the true faith, Eastern Orthodoxy, to the West and to develop a new civilization compounded of the best both Russia and the West had to offer. Pan-Slavism propounded a federation of five Slavic states under Russian dominance, to be achieved by the liberation of the Slavic peoples.

Dostoevsky's experiences in life and the beliefs and attitudes that developed from them are reflected in *Crime and Punishment,* as they are in his other works. They are not the beliefs that would ordinarily evolve in a man who has experienced near-execution, imprisonment, poverty, and physical and mental suffering during most of his life. For, rather than disillusionment and despair, these experiences brought to Dostoevsky joy, faith, and acceptance of life.

It is this view that permeates *Crime and Punishment.* Despite the intense sufferings that Raskolnikov endures through most of the book, his final vision is not one of despair but of infinite hope. Never once does Dostoevsky indict Raskolnikov. Along every step of the young man's path away from, and then toward, regeneration, Dostoevsky *understands* him. He understood him because he himself had endured deep sufferings throughout most of his own life. It is this great sense of reality he gave to his writings that ranks Dostoevsky as one of literature's geniuses.

Plot Summary

Crime and Punishment is one of the greatest stories of psychological suspense ever written, but the plot is very simple. Rodion Romanovitch Raskolnikov, a poor student, kills an old woman, a pawnbroker, to prove that he is a kind of superman not subject to moral law. Unlike familiar murder stories, there is no pursuit and no capture. No evidence links the student with the crime. However, after he has committed the murder, Raskolnikov's conscience begins to suffer and he becomes increasingly unstable—physically, emotionally, and mentally. Because Raskolnikov had pawned something with the murdered woman, he is routinely questioned by the police. The chief inspector, Porfiry Petrovitch, is very perceptive, and his suspicions about Raskolnikov are soon aroused. The two men meet several times again, and Porfiry finally becomes convinced that Raskolnikov is the murderer. Rather than arrest him, Porfiry gives Raskolnikov time to confess his crime voluntarily. Porfiry sees Raskolnikov as a brilliant but misguided young man, and believes that a voluntary confession would be the first essential step toward his regeneration.

After a long period of anguished indecision, Raskolnikov is persuaded by Sonia, the woman he loves, to confess his crime. Sonia sees Raskolnikov as a child of God, and in her simple religious way wants him to rediscover God. She faithfully follows Raskolnikov to Siberia after his trial, and through her patient and quiet devotion Raskolnikov is finally able to learn humility, gain faith in God, and begin a new life with her.

Characters in the Novel

Dushkin: A peasant who gives evidence regarding the painters Nikolay and Dmitri.

Nikodim Fomich: Superintendent of the district police in St. Petersburg.

Amalia Fyodorovna: Landlady of Marmeladov and his family, alternately the enemy of Katerina Ivanovna.

Alyona Ivanovna: Old pawnbroker whom Raskolnikov murders in cold blood.

Katerina Ivanovna: Despairing wife of the shiftless Marmeladov. Katerina dies of consumption, leaving her children, Polenka, Lida and Kolya, orphans.

Lizaveta Ivanovna: 35-year-old half-sister of Alyona Ivanovna and friend of Sonia. She is killed by Raskolnikov.

Kapernaumov: Cleft-palated tailor in whose house Sonia lodges after her disgrace.

Koch and Pestryakov: Innocent suspects in the murders.

Andrey Semyonovitch Lebeziatnikov: Intellectual and free-thinker who lodges in the same house as the Marmeladovs.

Peter Petrovitch Luzhin: A boorish gentleman betrothed to Dounia for his money, then rejected by her.

Semyon Zaharovitch Marmeladov: Fallen civil servant who drinks away his second chance and causes his family's ruin.

Sofya Semyonovna Marmeladov (Sonia): The almost saintly stepdaughter of Marmeladov, who prostitutes herself to feed her family and becomes Raskolnikov's lifeline to humanity.

Mikolka: Cruel figure in Raskolnikov's dream who beats his mare to death for fun.

Nikolay Dementyev and Dmitri: Suspects in the murders.

Praskovya Pavlovna: Raskolnikov's tormenting landlady.

Porfiry Petrovitch: The intelligent police investigator who finally deduces that Raskolnikov is the murderer.

Nastasya Nikiforovna Petrovna: Servant of Praskovya Pavlovna, Nastasya attends Raskolnikov.

Marfa Petrovna: Ill-fated wife of Svidrigailov, who is rumored to have murdered her.

Pokorev: Student who introduces Raskolnikov to Alyona Ivanovna.

Avdotya Raskolnikov (Dounia): Raskolnikov's sister, who is pursued by Luzhin and Svidrigailov.

Pulcheria Raskolnikov: Raskolnikov's impoverished mother.

Rodion Romanovitch Raskolnikov (Rodya, etc.): Brilliant university student who must leave off his study because he has no money. On the verge of madness, he murders Alyona and Liza-veta Ivanovna, then faces the consequences of his crime.

Dmitri Prokofitch Razumihin (or Vrazumihin):   Raskolnikov's impulsive friend who is attracted to Dounia.

Resslich: A foreigner whose teenage deaf-and-dumb niece commits suicide by hanging herself.

Arkady Ivanovitch Svidrigailov: A wealthy, sophisticated, and evil person who is attracted to Dounia. When she rejects him, he commits suicide.

Vassily Ivanovitch Vahrushin: The merchant who lends Pulcheria Raskolnikov money.

Zametov: Police clerk and acquaintance of Razumihin.

Zossimov: The physician who attends Raskolnikov.

Note: The above list by no means exhausts the hundreds of characters who appear in the novel. Complete names and nicknames are given where the figures are called by various names and may be confused with others.

Russian Names

In Russian, proper names are made up of three parts: the first, or baptismal name; the middle name, or patronymic; and the last, or family name. The patronymic is composed of the first name of the person's father plus either the suffix *ovitch*, to denote "son of," or *ovna*, to denote "daughter of." The father of Rodion and Avdotya was named *Roman*, and thus Rodion's patronymic, or middle name, is *Romanovitch*, and Avdotya's is *Romanovna*.

The last, or family, name is the same for both men and women with the exception that sometimes the family name is feminized for a daughter. Thus, Avdotya's last name could also be *Raskolnikovna*. The usual way of addressing another person is to use both the baptismal name and the patronymic together as, for example, *Rodion Romanovitch*.

There are two major exceptions to this form. First, certain persons such as servants or others whom one would tend to regard with informality are most usually called only by their first names. Nastasya, the servant girl of Praskovya Pavlovna, is always simply "Nastasya." Second, within families and between close friends, diminutives, the equivalents of nicknames, are most often used.

Introduction

Because much of the action in *Crime and Punishment* is internal, many of the external happenings seem to have occupied less of the author's attention. At least two of the crucial events, for example, rely on coincidence. Raskolnikov accidentally overhears Lizaveta make an appointment with some hucksters for seven o'clock the next evening, which will leave the old pawnbroker alone and so present him with the opportunity for the murder. Svidrigailov happens to be a boarder in the same house as Sonia and chances to overhear Raskolnikov confess the crime to her. Many chapters end with the sudden, and often unexpected, appearance of a character whose arrival mechanically sets up the framework for the following chapter.

How does this structure affect the novel? In a lesser story, such an obvious mechanical structure might annoy and distract the reader. But in *Crime and Punishment* this does not occur, for the framework becomes secondary to the story's superb characterization.

Dostoevsky is noted for profound insights into his characters who, revealed to their core, stand among the memorable creations in literature. Unforgettable, for example, are the pathetic Marmeladov, his distraught wife, the amoral Svidrigailov, the good friend Razumihin, and the astute Porfiry, all of whom are firmly etched in lifelike detail.

The one outstanding exception, perhaps, is Sonia. Although Sonia plays a major role in the drama and is *deep* enough to match Raskolnikov's depths, she tends also to be *flat*. That is, she has but one side: an all-consuming, angelic goodness. There is no instance in the book in which Sonia is portrayed otherwise. Had she been given some flaw, she would be less unearthly and perhaps as convincingly real to us as the other characters that populate the novel.

The central theme of *Crime and Punishment* is that man, no matter how tainted by evil, can be reborn and achieve salvation through faith in God. This theme expresses Dostoevsky's own religious belief. In the novel, the theme is expressed most fully in the character of Rodion Raskolnikov, the central figure.

Salvation, as Dostoevsky describes it in *Crime and Punishment,* can be achieved by rejecting pride, confessing one's sins, and accepting suffering. The novel begins with Raskolnikov embroiled in a web of pride: his theory of the "extraordinary man." Until the very end of the book Raskolnikov holds the pride of his conviction that his theory may be valid, that the "proof" failed only because he, as an individual, was too weak an instrument to "step over barriers" with impunity. Only during his imprisonment does he finally realize that he is wrong.

Even before this evolution of Raskolnikov's spirit is completed, however, he confesses his guilt, although he does not *believe* it, and so accepts his suffering. The impulse to confess begins just after he commits the murder. Hiding in the slain moneylender's apartment, he is tempted "to end it all at once and shout" to the unexpected visitors knocking on the door. At various other times throughout the story, the possibility of confession is considered but then rejected by Raskolnikov. At one point he decides to confess and experiences a joy in life such as he has not felt in many months. He sees in confession the key to regeneration and salvation, but is unable to take the deciding step toward it because his pride could not bear the humility he would have to endure in confessing his crime. Still later, he tests the depths of Sonia's capacity to share his suffering. Only after he is convinced that her own faith in God is unshakable and that she would be able to bear his suffering in addition to her own does he allow himself to confess to her. Her love toward Raskolnikov, an expression of God's love toward all men, opens the door to his own salvation.

As Raskolnikov struggles upward toward salvation he is drawn alternately between the poles of good on the one hand and evil on the other. His nature is the same dual nature, Dostoevsky says, that is in every man. Razumihin once described Raskolnikov as appearing to be "alternating between two characters." Manifestations of this duality are evident in many ways. Among them are his crystal-clear thinking when confronting Porfiry, as contrasted with his usually confused state of mind; his intellectual desire to prove his theory versus his emotional impulse to confess; and his alternating compassion and cruelty. The forces of good and evil that contend for his soul are represented outwardly by Sonia and Svidrigailov, each of whom is drawn to Raskolnikov and tries to control him.

Raskolnikov encounters Sonia first, early in the story. Sonia, the angelic personification of Christian love, sacrifice, suffering, and humility, believes wholly in the power of God to save men. Svidrigailov appears later in the story. From the first, he observes that there is a mysterious attraction between the young student and himself, and at one point he calls himself and Raskolnikov "birds of a feather." Raskolnikov never hesitates to make it clear to Svidrigailov that he suspects him of the most evil intentions. Yet he seeks him out because he feels that Svidrigailov has "some hidden power over him." The extent of this power is seen near the end of the book, when Raskolnikov overhears in the police station that Svidrigailov has committed suicide. At that moment Raskolnikov feels "as though something had fallen on him and was stifling him." It is as though a part of him, too, has been killed.

Sonia has read to Raskolnikov the Biblical story of Lazarus who was raised from the dead by Jesus and, like Lazarus, Raskolnikov himself is raised from spiritual death to new life. In contrast, Svidrigailov, empty of spirit, totally alone and unloved, kills himself. Accepting God's love, Raskolnikov's dual nature becomes whole: through faith he has achieved oneness.

Raskolnikov, like most of mankind, but to a greater degree than most, is isolated from himself, from his fellow man, and from God. He remains in a state of isolation for as long as his pride remains with him. Only when he finally rejects his pride, or "self," does he gain the capacity to embrace others. Dostoevsky seems to be saying that through a similar act of self-negation all people can end their isolation and reach out to one another.

Chapter by Chapter Summaries and Commentaries

PART I • CHAPTER 1

The Plan
Summary

It is a hot July evening in St. Petersburg, Russia, in the mid-nineteenth century. A young man leaves his garret room for a walk outdoors and succeeds in slipping unnoticed past the open door of his landlady's quarters. The young man is a university student but has recently left school because he lacks the money to continue. "For some time past he had been in an over-strained, irritable condition, verging on hypochondria." His thoughts frequently center about an undefined "that": "Am I capable of *that*?" he thinks to himself. The young man is "exceptionally handsome, above average in height, slim, well-built, with beautiful dark eyes and dark brown hair." He has had almost nothing to eat during the past two days, and he is very shabbily dressed. However, his heart is so filled with "accumulated bitterness and contempt" that he is not concerned about his appearance.

Suddenly a huge wagon lumbers by and a drunken man in it shouts at him, "Hey there, German hatter!" referring to the peculiar style of the young man's hat. He is shaken, not from shame, but in a way that seems somehow related to the mysterious "that." "I thought so!" he mutters. "Why, a stupid thing like this, the most trivial detail might spoil the whole plan. . . . Nobody wears such a hat, it would be noticed a mile off, it would be remembered." The young man continues walking, and we learn that he already knows the exact number of steps to his destination. It suddenly dawns on him that he is actually carrying out a "rehearsal" of his "project"—"at every step his excitement grew more and more violent."

He reaches a huge house and climbs the stairs to the fourth floor. He rings the bell of a flat (apartment), and the door is opened a crack by an old woman. After eyeing him suspiciously, she lets him in. The woman has "sharp malignant eyes," and she "coughed and groaned at every instant." The young man identifies himself: "Raskolnikov, a student, I came here a month ago." The old woman is Alyona Ivanovna, a pawnbroker, and the young man has brought a silver watch to pawn. While the woman is completing the transaction, Raskolnikov quickly but carefully studies her, the apartment, and her possessions. At one point he notices the sunlight in the room and thinks, "So the sun will shine like this *then* too!" Before leaving, the young man says that he will bring something else to pawn in a few days.

He departs in an agitated state, and when he is on the street again, he wonders, "How could such an atrocious thing come into my head?" He goes into a tavern and orders some beer. His mind becomes clearer and he shrugs off his thoughts as "nonsense." As he sits and looks around him, Raskolnikov's eye is drawn to another man in the tavern, a man also somewhat agitated, who appears to be "a retired government clerk."

Commentary

Raskolnikov's avoidance of his landlady is the first indication of his isolation from others. His isolation will become one of the major themes of the book.

Dostoevsky was a city-dweller most of his life (he lived for many years in St. Petersburg). In the original work, you will see his great ability to describe in detail the cluttered rooms and narrow streets found in many cities.

St. Petersburg, also once known as Petersburg and later as Petrograd, is now called Leningrad.

When Raskolnikov discusses with the moneylender the amount of money he is to receive for the silver watch, they talk in terms of *roubles* and *copecks*. The rouble was, and is, the basic unit in the Russian monetary system. There are 100 copecks in one rouble; the rouble is worth approximately $1.00, American currency.

QUESTION: In the midst of his disturbed thoughts, Raskolnikov makes a seemingly unrelated reference to "Jack the Giant-killer." Does this provide a clue about the mysterious "*that*"?

CHAPTER 2

Marmeladov
Summary

In the tavern, Raskolnikov keeps looking at the clerk, and the clerk returns his stares. The clerk is "a man over fifty, bald and grizzled, of medium height, and stoutly built." His face is "bloated from continual drinking." However, the most noticeable thing about him is the "intense feeling" in his eyes. The clerk begins to speak to Raskolnikov. He introduces himself as Marmeladov and announces grandly that he is "a titular counsellor in rank." He continues to speak in a style not at all in character with his appearance or the surroundings. Marmeladov talks in the most familiar manner about his personal life. He admits that he is a hopeless drunk and even describes himself as a "pig" and "beast." He tells Raskolnikov that he has stolen and sold articles of his wife's clothing in order to obtain money for drink. In the past winter he sold her shawl, and as a result she caught cold and is now coughing severely and spitting blood. His wife,

Katerina Ivanovna, "is at work from morning till night; she is scrubbing and cleaning and washing the children." Marmeladov cries out, "Do you suppose I don't feel it? And the more I drink the more I feel it."

Marmeladov says that his wife was a widow with three children when he married her. For an entire year he was able to abstain from drinking, but in the past half year he has begun again to take up his old habit. Sonia, his daughter by his first wife, has been forced to become a prostitute in order to supply the family with money. Five weeks before, however, Marmeladov had obtained a new position. His family had been ecstatic, treating him with new respect, and looking forward to a bright future. All had gone well until five nights before, when "like a thief in the night, I stole from Katerina Ivanovna the key of her box, took out what was left of my earnings, how much it was I have forgotten, and now look at me!" Marmeladov suddenly rises unsteadily and tells Raskolnikov to come along with him—he is going to return home. They leave the tavern and make their way to his fourth-floor apartment.

The room is described as "about ten paces long" and lit up by "a candle end." It is cluttered with rags, has a few shabby pieces of furniture, and appears to be little more than a hallway that leads to a larger room in the rear, where some people are boisterously playing cards and partying. Katerina Ivanovna is walking back and forth, her hands clasped to her chest, and "her eyes glittered as in fever and looked about with a harsh immovable stare." At first she sees only Raskolnikov, but then she spies Marmeladov kneeling in the doorway and screams, "He has come back! The criminal! The monster! And where is the money?" Furious, she grabs his hair and pulls him into the room. Thinking that Raskolnikov has been her husband's drinking companion, Katerina Ivanovna turns upon him and orders him away. As he leaves, Raskolnikov takes some money from his pocket and puts it on the window sill. On the stairway he stops and thinks, "What a stupid thing I've done." But then he dismisses the money "with a wave of his hand."

Commentary

Marmeladov describes Sonia as "a gentle creature with a soft little voice . . . fair hair and such a pale, thin little face." Note the discreet manner in which Dostoevsky discloses the fact that she is a prostitute. Marmeladov never says it directly, but refers to a "yellow ticket" and a "yellow passport" that she has. This is a reference to the yellow cards that prostitutes were required to carry.

Remember that Sonia is Marmeladov's daughter from his first marriage, so that although Katerina Ivanovna is referred to throughout as her mother, she is actually her stepmother.

When describing his suffering Marmeladov states, "I accept it all, not with contempt, but with humility. . . . 'Behold the man!' " In the Bible (John 19:5) Pilate says "Behold the man!" when Jesus appears before him wearing the crown of thorns. Marmeladov is comparing his own suffering and humility with Christ's.

Marmeladov describes his wife as having "a tendency to consumption." The word *consumption* was once widely used for the disease we now call tuberculosis.

In this chapter we learn that a person named Amalia Fyodorovna Lippevechsel is the Marmeladovs' landlady. Speaking of her house, Marmeladov calls it "a perfect Bedlam." Bedlam is a common reference to any wild uproar; it is derived from the name of the St. Mary of Bethlehem Hospital in London, long used as a hospital for lunatics.

We also learn that "Semyon Zaharovitch" are Marmeladov's first two names.

In one passage Marmeladov imagines Judgment Day and refers to "the Image of the Beast," which is a reference to the devil.

When Raskolnikov and Marmeladov climb the stairs to the latter's apartment, "it was nearly eleven o'clock and although in summer in Petersburg there is no real night, yet it was quite dark at the top of the stairs." Leningrad is only about 500 miles south of the Arctic Circle and lies on the same latitude as Oslo, Norway, and Seward, Alaska. It has the same long winter nights and long summer days as other far northern cities. At the time of the story it is summer and the period of the "white nights."

The close of this chapter points up one of Raskolnikov's basic conflicts—his emotional desire to do good versus his intellectual conviction to remain aloof from such feelings. He gives his last money to Katerina Ivanovna and then immediately judges his act as a "stupid thing."

QUESTION: What kind of man do you think Marmeladov is?

CHAPTER 3

The Letter
Summary
It is the next day. Raskolnikov wakes up "ill-tempered." Nastasya, employed by the landlady as a cook and servant, enters the young student's tiny, littered room to clean it up. She tells Raskolnikov that his landlady, Praskovya Pavlovna, is going to the police because he has not paid his rent for so long. This upsets him greatly. They talk, and Nastasya blames Raskolnikov for thinking too much and working too little. Then Nastasya remembers that a letter came for him the previous day. "Then bring it to me, . . . bring it," he cries.

The letter, from his mother, takes up almost all the rest of the chapter. It recounts the experiences of his mother and sister during the preceding two months. His sister, Dounia, had been employed as a governess in the house of a man named Svidrigailov. He had treated her rudely and eventually made a "shameful proposal" to her, which he repeated from time to time. Mr. Svidrigailov's wife, Marfa Petrovna, came upon them during one such occasion and immediately thought that Dounia was seducing her husband. She banished Dounia from the house. Later, Mr. Svidrigailov admitted that he had been the sole cause of the trouble, and his wife had taken great pains to go about the village and set the story straight. At about this time, a successful lawyer, Pyotr Petrovitch Luzhin, became very interested in Dounia and now, writes Raskolnikov's mother, Dounia and Luzhin are going to be married. She indicates that Dounia does not really love the man, but the girl believes that the security this marriage offers will be beneficial to her mother and brother. Furthermore, they are all coming to Petersburg soon.

In the letter his mother asks Raskolnikov more than once to try to understand Luzhin when they meet; not to pre-judge him, but to try to see his virtues as well as his faults. She has also reminded her son several times how very much his sister loves him, indeed, even "more than herself," and that "you are everything to us." Raskolnikov begins reading the letter in tears; but by the time he finishes it, "a bitter, wrathful and malignant smile was on his lips." Raskolnikov leaves his small room and goes out talking aloud to himself.

Commentary

At the beginning of her letter, Raskolnikov's mother addresses him as "Rodya." This is a familiar endearment for his first name, Rodion.

When she was sent home in the open cart, Dounia had to travel "seventeen versts." A verst is a Russian measure of length equal to about two-thirds of a mile.

The night before Dounia finally decided to agree to marry Luzhin, she prayed before an "icon." An icon (often spelled "ikon") is a religious representation, such as a painting or mosaic, of Christ, the Virgin Mary, or a saint.

QUESTION: Why do you think Raskolnikov's face is twisted into a bitter smile when he finishes reading the letter?

CHAPTER 4

A Walk
Summary

"Never such a marriage while I am alive and Mr. Luzhin be

damned!" blurts out Raskolnikov to himself. "No, mother, no, Dounia, you won't deceive me!" His smile had been one of decision, for all the while that he had been reading the letter he had become more and more determined that his sister would not marry Luzhin. On the one hand, his mother seemed to believe that Luzhin was a generous man, that Dounia wanted to marry him, and that the marriage and consequent financial security would help Raskolnikov too. He, on the other hand, sees Luzhin as a wily miser who wants to acquire Dounia as he would a piece of property, and a man that he, Raskolnikov, would hate at first sight. He believes that he is right in his evaluation as he recollects portions of his mother's letter. A man "who *seems* to be kind," his mother had written. "That *seems* beats everything!" Raskolnikov says. "Dounia for that very *'seems'* is marrying him!" His mother had also expressed gratitude that Luzhin had offered to send their bags ahead for them. "That was something, wasn't it, to send the bags and big box for them! A kind man, no doubt, after that! But his *bride* and her mother are to drive in a peasant's cart" at their own expense.

Raskolnikov believes he knows why Dounia has agreed to the marriage. It is because his sister, as his mother has written, "loves you more than herself." As much as he hates the idea of the marriage, he suddenly pauses and asks himself what right he has to say no. Feeling anguished that he cannot provide for his mother and sister himself, he decides that he can no longer remain passive but that "he must do something, do it at once, and do it quickly." The thought that had occupied him the evening before recurs, but "now it appeared not a dream at all, it had taken a new, menacing and quite unfamiliar shape."

Raskolnikov looks up and sees a young girl in front of him. He realizes that she is drunk and has been "deceived." On the other side of the street is a "plump, thickly-set man" who has apparently been following the girl. "Hey! What do you want here?" Raskolnikov shouts. The young student sees a policeman and persuades him to keep an eye on the girl. However, as the policeman walks after the girl, Raskolnikov shouts after him, "Let them be! What is it to do with you? Let her go! Let him amuse himself." He wonders to himself whether it was any business of his to interfere. "Let them devour each other alive—what is it to me?" he says. Raskolnikov's thoughts unexpectedly turn to one of his old friends at the university, Razumihin, whom he has not seen for four months. He realizes that when he had left his room earlier he had really intended to visit Razumihin.

Commentary

When thinking of his sister praying before the icon, Raskolnikov

16

had exclaimed, "Bitter is the ascent to Golgotha." This is a reference to the place outside Jerusalem where Christ was crucified. Golgotha also denotes any place of martyrdom, and perhaps this generality is what Raskolnikov had in mind.

Raskolnikov describes his mother as one of those with "Schilleresque noble hearts" who "hope for the best and will see nothing wrong." Johann Christoph Friedrich von Schiller (1759-1805) was one of Germany's greatest literary figures. Many of his writings exemplify his idealism and ethical principles. In his early works, Schiller's heroes are idealists crushed by villainous opponents. Raskolnikov evidently sees his mother and sister in just such a situation.

Contemplating his sister's moral firmness, Raskolnikov knows that she would not sell herself "for all Schleswig-Holstein." Now a state of West Germany, Schleswig-Holstein in the mid-nineteenth century was a territory bitterly fought over by Denmark and Germany. Raskolnikov also feels that Dounia would rather be a "Lett with a German master" than marry. The Letts are a people closely associated with Latvia. For centuries Latvia had been dominated by a class of German merchants that had reduced the native Letts to serfdom. A "Lett with a German master" would probably be a very miserable person.

Looking at the young girl being followed by the plump man, Raskolnikov thinks with extreme irony, "That's as it should be, they tell us. A certain percentage, they tell us, must every year go . . . to the devil. . . . Once you've said 'percentage,' there's nothing more to worry about." He is referring to the avant-garde thoughts of the day regarding scientific and social determinism—that man is destined to his fate.

QUESTION: When Raskolnikov wonders whether he would be able to provide a better future for his family than Luzhin would, he calls himself "oh, future millionaire Zeus." Is this an ironic statement? What does it mean?

CHAPTER 5

The Dream
Summary
Razumihin is a good-natured young man, very intelligent, very strong, and able to live entirely on what he can earn from small jobs. Raskolnikov considers going to see Razumihin, to find out if his friend can get him some kind of work. But then Raskolnikov decides to see him later, "on the next day after It," "when It will be over and everything will begin afresh." He walks into the countryside on the outskirts of the city, where he finds a tavern; he goes in and drinks a

glass of vodka. On his way home he turns off the road, lies down, and quickly falls asleep.

Raskolnikov has a terrible dream. He dreams that he is a little boy again, walking with his father in the country. As they pass a tavern they see a heavy cart, the kind usually drawn by a big work horse. In the shafts of this cart is "a thin little sorrel beast." Suddenly there is a lot of shouting and a group of people come from the tavern. One of them, Mikolka, the owner of the sorrel, urges them all to climb into the cart. "I'll make her gallop!" he says as he picks up the whip. They all join in whipping and flogging the poor beast about the body and eyes. The boy in the dream runs to the horse, crying. Mikolka, unable to make the horse move, beats her with a wooden shaft and then an iron crowbar until she falls to the ground dying. Someone calls for an axe to finish her off. The boy screams and puts his arms around the head of the dead animal, kissing its eyes and lips. Choking, the boy tries to breathe, and then Raskolnikov wakes up. "Good God," he cries, "can it be, can it be, that I shall really take an axe, that I shall strike her on the head, split her skull open . . . that I shall tread in the sticky warm blood, break the lock, steal and tremble; hide, all spattered in the blood. . . ." He shudders from the effect of the dream, but after he prays "Lord, show me my path—I renounce that accursed . . . dream of mine," he feels a sudden freedom from his obsession.

He continues his way toward home, not by the shortest route but, unconsciously, by a longer way. In a marketplace called the Hay Market he happens to come upon two hucksters talking with Lizaveta Ivanovna, the younger stepsister of Alyona Ivanovna, the pawnbroker. Unnoticed, he is able to listen to their conversation and learns that Lizaveta is planning to return to the market on the following night at seven o'clock. Quite by chance he has found out, without risky questioning, that the old pawnbroker, "on whose life an attempt was contemplated, would be at home and entirely alone." When he reaches his room Raskolnikov feels like a "man condemned to death." The sense of freedom he had enjoyed briefly after his dream has vanished. It is as though "he had no more freedom of thought . . . and that everything was suddenly and irrevocably decided."

Commentary

When Raskolnikov walks toward the outskirts of the city he goes across the "Vassilyevsky Ostrov." *Ostrov* is a Russian word for *island*. Vassilyevsky Ostrov is one of the islands of the delta that the river Neva has formed as its mouth.

The dream and Raskolnikov's reaction to it, as described in this chapter, are good examples of the kind of psychological analysis that Dostoevsky has undertaken in *Crime and Punishment*. It helps explain why this book has been called one of literature's greatest psychological novels. The dream is a symbolic portrayal of Raskolnikov's dual nature. In it, he is both the cruel Mikolka and the sympathetic boy. Raskolnikov's duality will be discussed later in the book.

QUESTION: When Raskolnikov returns homeward after his dream he goes by a route that is actually out of the way. The question here is one that Raskolnikov will later ask himself: Why had he gone that way at "the very minute of his life when he was just in the very mood and in the very circumstances in which that meeting was able to exert the gravest and most decisive influence on his whole destiny"? Could it be coincidence?

CHAPTER 6

The Plan Unfolds
Summary

Six weeks before, Raskolnikov had seen the old pawnbroker for the first time when he left a ring with her. At that first meeting he had felt a great repulsion toward her. After he left her apartment he had gone to a tavern and happened to sit next to a student and a young officer. It had given him an "extraordinary impression" when he overheard them speaking of Alyona Ivanovna, the very woman he had just visited! Raskolnikov listened to them talk about Alyona and her stepsister, Lizaveta.

The student was propounding a theory: It would certainly be beneficial, he maintained, to do away with that one terrible old woman and use her money to help hundreds of others who needed it more. "Kill her, take her money and with the help of it devote oneself to the service of humanity and the good of all." When Raskolnikov had heard this he had been "violently agitated . . . why had he happened to hear such a discussion and such ideas at the very moment when his own brain was just conceiving . . . *the very same idea*?"

The story now returns to the present. After Raskolnikov had overheard Lizaveta and the hucksters in the Hay Market, he went to bed and slept fitfully until early the next evening. He wakes to hear the clock strike. He knows it is late and leaps from his bed. Quickly, he takes an old shirt, tears strips from it, and fashions a sling that he sews under his overcoat. He has planned to conceal the axe there—the axe that he will secretly take from the landlady's kitchen below. He then takes from its hiding place the piece of wood and metal, securely wrapped, that he will give the old woman to pawn.

Quietly, he goes down to the kitchen, but is shocked to see that Nastasya is there hanging up some wash. He is furious with himself for having counted on no one being in the kitchen. Perplexed, he pauses near the gateway of the house. He happens to look into the porter's room, and there, under a bench, is an axe. No one is around, and

Raskolnikov takes the axe, secures it in the sling under his overcoat, and makes his way to the pawnbroker's house. He climbs the stairs cautiously, unseen by two painters, and rings the bell. There is no answer. He puts his ear to the door. He can hear someone on the other side, listening as he is. Finally, the door latch is unfastened.

Commentary

At the restaurant the student had said to the young officer: "Oh, well, brother, but we have to correct and direct nature, and, but for that, we should drown in an ocean of prejudice. But for that, there would never have been a single great man." When the student says that "we have to correct and direct nature" he means that men must take things into their own hands or they will be overwhelmed ("drowned") by the blind forces of nature (the "ocean of prejudice").

Pay special attention to the next sentence: "But for that, there would never have been a single great man." This sums up the seed of a theory that Raskolnikov later expounds, and one that forms a central part of the story.

On his way to the pawnbroker's Raskolnikov passes "the Yusupov garden," "the field of Mars," and "the Mihailovsky Palace." All three locations are clustered together on the southern bank of the Neva near the present Kirov Bridge. The Field of Mars is now a large grassy park known as the Square of the Revolution. Just to the west of the park are the Mihailovsky garden and the Mihailovsky Palace, both of which still exist. Leningrad contains many such grand buildings and parks. The city was founded in 1703 by Peter the Great (hence, "Petersburg"), who envisioned it as a great capital city.

QUESTION: Is *Crime and Punishment* more believable because it takes place in an actual city rather than in an imaginary place?

CHAPTER 7

The Murder
Summary

Raskolnikov strides into the room, alarming the old pawnbroker. She eyes him suspiciously but takes the package that he offers her. As she turns to the window to untie the string, Raskolnikov loosens the axe under his coat and holds it in his hand. When she turns back to him, Raskolnikov strikes her on the skull and kills her. He takes her keys from her pocket and, from a string around her neck, a heavy purse, noticing that two small crosses also hang from the string. He goes into her bedroom and there, in a box under the bed, discovers a number of pawned articles that he stuffs into his pockets. Suddenly he hears steps and when he rushes out of the bedroom he sees Lizaveta standing in the middle of the other room, horrified at the sight of her murdered stepsister. Raskolnikov kills her with the axe and rushes out into the hallway.

He returns to wipe the blood from his hands, his boots, and the axe. As he goes to leave again he stops in horror, for he sees that the pawnbroker had left the front door open! Hearing someone ascending the stairs, he closes the door and secures the latch. A man rings for the pawnbroker. Soon another man joins him. The men converse outside and become suspicious because no one answers. One goes for the porter but is slow in returning, and the second, impatient, also goes downstairs. Raskolnikov makes his way down to the second floor. He hears shouting below him, followed by the sound of several men hurrying up the stairs. He spies the empty room that has just been vacated by the painters and hides there as the men go up to the pawnbroker's apartment. Raskolnikov arrives home safely, though shaken, returns the axe to the porter's quarters, and then sinks onto his bed, his head swimming with thoughts.

Commentary

In the previous chapter Raskolnikov had thought it was obvious that criminals were caught because they lost their reason and willpower when committing their crime. He had "decided that in his own case there could not be such a morbid reaction, that his reason and will would remain unimpaired at the time of carrying out his design." However, after committing his crime he is astounded to see that he has made one of the most obvious blunders—he has not closed the door that Alyona had left open.

As he takes the purse from around Alyona's neck, Raskolnikov notices that she wears two crosses on the same string, one of copper and the other "of Cyprus [i.e. cypress] wood." Much later in the novel Raskolnikov learns that Sonia, Marmeladov's daughter, possesses these crosses. Still later, she will give one of them to Raskolnikov.

One of this novel's central themes is that of confession, and through confession the attainment of salvation. Although it will take Raskolnikov until the end of the novel before he is finally able to confess his guilt, the first thought of confession appears in this chapter. Hiding from the two men behind the door, Raskolnikov thinks "to end it all at once and shout to them through the door." However he does not "end it all" then, and his continuing inability to do so becomes one of the novel's major themes.

QUESTION: Remembering the reasons Raskolnikov uses to justify his murder of Alyona, how do you think he can justify his murder of Lizaveta?

PART II • CHAPTER 1

At the Police Station
Summary

Raskolnikov lies quite dazed through most of the night. At the first light of morning he examines his clothes for blood stains. He sees some at the bottom of his trousers and cuts them off with a knife. Then he stuffs the small packages he has taken from the pawnbroker into a hole in the wall behind some loose wallpaper. He remembers the sling, tears it from inside his overcoat, and thrusts the pieces of rag under his pillow. A sudden ray of sunlight on his boot exposes more blood, and he finds some inside a pocket. Plagued by chills and fever, his mind in a frenzy, he falls asleep again, clutching the bloody shreds of his trousers and his blood-stained sock.

A knocking on the door wakes him up. It is Nastasya with the house porter, who hands him a sealed paper and says that it is a summons from the police. Raskolnikov is not sure why the police want him, and suspects that he may be "lost." He goes to the police station, and as he approaches it he thinks, "If they question me, perhaps I'll simply tell."

At the police station he has to wait a while and no one seems particularly interested in the fact of his presence. He finally learns that the police have been asked to recover money Raskolnikov owes his landlady. He has been called to the station to write out a declaration stating when he intends to pay her. The proceedings at the station are interrupted by the arrival of Nikodim Fomitch, the district police superintendent. Fomitch seems sympathetic toward Raskolnikov, and after writing out his declaration Raskolnikov is impelled for a moment to tell him all that happened the night before. As he rises to do so, he hears Fomitch talking with the chief clerk about the murder of the old pawnbroker. Raskolnikov starts for the door to leave, but he collapses. When he regains consciousness Nikodim Fomitch is standing near, "looking intently at him." The assistant superintendent, Ilya Petrovitch, begins to question Raskolnikov. The young student briefly reveals that he had been ill on the previous day, that he had gone out about seven, and that he had gone "along the street." "Short and clear," says the assistant superintendent. "There was a sudden silence." "Very well, then," states Ilya Petrovitch, "we will not detain you." As Raskolnikov leaves he hears hurried conversation behind him. "The brutes! They suspect."

Commentary

We will learn later that Raskolnikov's statements and actions at the police station *have* placed him under suspicion.

Note that once again Raskolnikov has a recurring desire to confess, and almost does so to the police superintendent.

QUESTION: When he awakens to discover blood on his clothes, Raskolnikov is highly confused and becomes convinced that he is losing his memory and his other senses. "Surely it isn't beginning already!" he says. "Surely it isn't my punishment coming upon me? It is!" If Raskolnikov had previously found no objection to committing the murder, why does he now expect to be punished for it?

CHAPTER 2

At Razumihin's
Summary

Raskolnikov goes from the police station to his room. Afraid that his room is going to be searched, he takes the small packages out of the hole in the wall where he has hidden them and puts them in his pockets. He goes to the canal where, in his delirium of the previous night, he felt he should dispose of this evidence. When he reaches the canal there are too many people about, and he turns instead toward the Neva. On his way there he spies a long alleyway leading to a courtyard. He decides to hide the stolen articles inside the courtyard entrance, and seizing a huge stone he turns it over, places the items in a small hollow in the ground beneath it, and rolls the stone back over it. He is filled with joy. "I have buried my tracks! . . . who can think of looking under that stone? . . . It is all over! No clue!" He wonders what was in the stolen purse which, strangely, he had not opened before placing it under the rock.

Raskolnikov suddenly stops and finds himself next to the house of his friend, Razumihin. He goes up to his friend's garret and is greeted by Razumihin, who sees that he is delirious. Razumihin offers to share some work he has received, translating a German text, and gives Raskolnikov the text and three roubles. Without a word the young student takes the text and the money and departs, but a few minutes later, just as silently, he returns and lays them again on the table. Raskolnikov leaves with a "Well, confound you then!" from Razumihin.

Out on the street again, Raskolnikov is lashed by a coachman for coming dangerously close to falling beneath his horses. A woman, feeling sorry for him, places twenty copecks in his hand. On the Nikolaevsky Bridge over the Neva, Raskolnikov opens his hand to stare at the coin and then hurls it into the water below. "It seemed to him, he had cut himself off from everyone and from everything at that moment."

Returning home, Raskolnikov sinks down onto his bed and loses consciousness. He is awakened by fearful screaming and hears his landlady being beaten on the stairs by the assistant police superintendent, Ilya Petrovitch. Raskolnikov wonders why Petrovitch has come. Soon after, Nastasya enters with some food, and Raskolnikov asks, "What were they beating the landlady for?" Nastasya looks at him intently for a long while. "Nobody has been beating the landlady," she says at last.

Commentary

Razumihin is translating texts for Heruvimov, who "is setting up for being advanced." This last phrase means that Heruvimov, a publisher, is having Razumihin translate texts far in advance of their being needed for publication.

Razumihin tells Raskolnikov that he has "two signatures" of the text. A signature is a printing term used to describe a printed sheet containing a designated number of pages.

When Raskolnikov pauses to look at the cathedral he recalls that when he attended the university, he had stood on the very spot, gazing, many times before, and always with a strange, lifeless feeling. He feels that it is no coincidence that at this particular moment he is there once again. He is repeating his old rejection of the cathedral, or God, once again, and it is at this moment that he hurls away the coin that the old lady had just given him, with the words "in Christ's name." One of the novel's great themes is Raskolnikov's initial rejection, and his final acceptance, of God.

QUESTION: Raskolnikov finds himself concentrating on a single "point." What do you think this "point" is? What do you think Raskolnikov means when he exclaims, "Damn it all! . . . If it has begun, then it has begun"?

CHAPTER 3

Razumihin Helps Raskolnikov
Summary

Raskolnikov continues to lie on his bed in a delirium. He is vaguely aware of people coming and going and making a good deal of fuss over him. Suddenly he comes to and sees Nastasya and a stranger standing before him. An instant later Razumihin enters. The stranger says that he is a messenger who has a remittance of 35 roubles from Raskolnikov's mother. Raskolnikov at first refuses to accept the money, but Razumihin finally manages to convince him to take it.

Razumihin is very talkative and in good spirits. He tells how he has inquired all around town to find Raskolnikov's room, and in the process has found out a great deal about him—"everything," in fact. He has made a fast friend of Praskovya Pavlovna, Raskolnikov's landlady, and is already calling her by her familiar name,

"Pashenka." In addition, he had brought both Zametov (the head clerk at the police station) and Dr. Zossimov to see Raskolnikov while he was delirious. Raskolnikov stares at his friend when he hears that Zametov has been there. "Did I say anything in delirium?" Raskolnikov asks. "I should think so!" replies Razumihin, and relates at length that he had seemed concerned about a "secret," about earrings, chains, and other items, including his sock. When Zametov had found the sock and given it to him, Raskolnikov had clutched it tightly.

After Razumihin and Nastasya leave, Raskolnikov checks the hole in the wall where he had originally hidden the packages. He finds the frayed ends of trousers in the stove just where he had left them, and sees that the sock, under his pillow, is too dirty to show any of the blood. Why has Razumihin brought Zametov and Dr. Zossimov to see him? Do they suspect? He must flee, Raskolnikov thinks, "far away . . . to America." He gulps down a half-full bottle of beer that Razumihin had left and soon falls asleep again in his bed.

Hours later Razumihin returns. He has been busy. He has been moving in with his uncle, in Raskolnikov's section of the city, and has also bought the young student some newer clothes with part of the money Raskolnikov received from his mother. He takes out of his bundle a new hat, trousers, and other clothes, making a great fuss over every item. When he offers to take off Raskolnikov's old rags to put on the new clothes, Raskolnikov refuses. Razumihin and Nastasya change him anyway. At that moment the door opens and a "tall, stout man" enters. "Zossimov! At last!" cries Razumihin.

Commentary

After Razumihin has asked Nastasya to bring him two bottles of beer he adds, "Cut along, Nastasya, and bring some tea, for tea we may venture on without the faculty." The meaning is that tea, unlike beer, can be drunk without any risk of losing one's faculty, or sense.

Dostoevsky writes an interesting description of "Nastasya, balancing a saucer on her five outspread fingers and sipping tea through a lump of sugar." Sipping liquids through a lump of sugar was once quite a treat, as was cutting a hole in an orange and sipping the juice through a lump of sugar.

At the police station, Raskolnikov had mentioned that he had once asked his landlady's daughter to marry him but that she had died. Here, we learn the girl's name—Natalya Yegorovna.

Razumihin states that he has brought the head police clerk, Zametov, to see Raskolnikov. We first met Zametov in Part II, Chapter I, where he is referred to only as Alexandr Grigorievitch. Zametov is his last name.

QUESTION: What do you think Raskolnikov means when, in his new clothes, he thinks, "It will be long before I get rid of them"? If you interpret this as a symbolic statement, do you think that Dostoevsky's symbol is a good one?

CHAPTER 4

Razumihin Discusses the Murder
Summary

Dr. Zossimov is a tall, fat, very fashionably dressed man, twenty-seven years old. He listens to Razumihin's report of Raskolnikov's state of health, watching Raskolnikov carefully. Razumihin asks him whether Raskolnikov would be able to attend a house-warming party he is giving that night and reminds Zossimov that he has promised to come. Zossimov asks him who else will be there and reacts with "I don't care a damn for him!" upon learning that Porfiry Petrovitch, "the head of the Investigation Department," will be there. Razumihin insists that Zossimov come anyway, mentions others who will be at the party, and generally continues to dominate the conversation.

Through his friend, Zametov, Razumihin has learned a good deal about the murder of the old pawnbroker, and he now discusses his theories about the case. He reveals that a house-painter, Nikolay, has been held as the murder suspect, but accuses the police of stupidly being misled by the most superficial of circumstances. "One can show from the psychological data alone how to get on the track of the real man," Razumihin insists. The painter (one of the two that Raskolnikov had seen in the old pawnbroker's house) had been picked up by the police after he had pawned some gold earrings. He had sworn that he had found them in a package in a corner near the door of the room where he and another man, Dmitri, had been working.

"Behind the door? Lying behind the door? Behind the door?" Raskolnikov suddenly cries with terror. There is a silence, and Razumihin looks "inquiringly at Zossimov." Razumihin then gives his version of the crime, accurately reconstructing what actually happened. Zossimov plainly doubts the story as "Too clever! . . . too melodramatic." At that moment the door opens and a stranger enters.

Commentary

In this chapter, we first hear the name of Porfiry Petrovitch, the head of the Investigation Department. Porfiry will play a major role in the novel and is one of its chief characters.

QUESTION: Do you think that Raskolnikov has aroused further suspicions with his outburst?

CHAPTER 5

Pyotr Petrovitch Luzhin

Summary

The person who enters is described as "no longer young, of a stiff and portly appearance, and a cautious and sour countenance." His affected mannerisms immediately arouse the antagonism of those assembled in the room. He announces that he is Pyotr Petrovitch Luzhin. At first, Raskolnikov looks at Luzhin as though he has never heard of him. Razumihin hastily explains that Raskolnikov has been ill and invites Luzhin into the already crowded room. Luzhin enters and, taking a seat, begins to explain in detail just who he is when Raskolnikov blurts out, "I know, I know! So you are the *fiancé*?" The newcomer is elegantly attired in fine, obviously new, summer clothes in youthful pastel shades, and his "very fresh and even handsome face looked younger than his forty-five years." However, his pomposity is quickly dissipated by the casual attitude of those in the room, and though their actions verge on impoliteness, he "hardened his heart and seemed to determine to take no notice of their oddities."

He continues his explanation, stating that he has found lodgings for Raskolnikov's mother and sister, Dounia, "in Bakaleyev's house." "I've been there. . . . A disgusting place," retorts Razumihin. Luzhin is again ruffled, but turns the conversation to "serious and essential matters," as he calls them. He begins a long discourse about their changing society and seems delighted with his own words. Zossimov has evidently been thinking of other things for he interrupts by saying, "One of her customers must have killed her." Razumihin takes up this new thread of conversation and reveals that Porfiry, the police detective, is "examining all who have pledges with her."

Raskolnikov attacks the ideas in Luzhin's lengthy discourse in the light of the murder, which, the student says to Luzhin, is "in accordance with your theory!" He continues his attack, quoting derogatory information about Luzhin from his mother's letter. "Luzhin turned pale and bit his lip," and as he stooped through the doorway to leave, "even the curve of his spine was expressive of the horrible insult he had received." Razumihin is perplexed at the vehemence of Raskolnikov's attack, but the young student only shouts, "Let me alone—let me alone, all of you!" When Razumihin and Zossimov leave, the former asks, "What's the matter with him?" Zossimov replies, "Have you noticed, . . . he does not respond to anything except one point on which he seems excited—that's the murder?" "Yes, yes," agrees Razumihin, "I noticed that, too."

Commentary

"Let me alone, all of you!" cries Raskolnikov. In addition to his separation from morality—brought to an extreme in his act of murder—the young student is now driving himself from society and his fellow man into a state of complete isolation.

Luzhin's "lavender gloves" are described as being "real Louvain." Louvain, a city in Belgium, was once a center of the cloth-weaving industry.

When Luzhin is analyzing the evolution of Russian society he says at one point, "Then the great hour struck." A footnote to this quote in the Constance Garnett translation says, "The emancipation of the serfs in 1861 is meant."

QUESTION: The question of coincidence has been raised earlier. Does it seem coincidental, in this chapter, that Luzhin is staying in the same house as Marmeladov, a man Raskolnikov already knows? Would you guess that this fact will play a significant role later on in the story?

CHAPTER 6

Raskolnikov Talks With Zametov
Summary

As soon as Razumihin, Zossimov, and Nastasya leave his room, Raskolnikov becomes "perfectly calm." He has made a decision that he will carry out "to-day, to-day." He dresses himself in the clothes Razumihin has brought, puts all his money in his pocket, and goes out with the "one thought only: 'that all *this* must be ended to-day, once and for all, immediately.' " Out on the street, Raskolnikov gives five copecks to a street singer and talks to a middle-aged man, a youth, and a prostitute because he feels "an unaccountable inclination to enter into conversation with people." He has read somewhere, he muses, that a man condemned to death would willingly stand "on a square yard of space" forever if only he could remain alive. "Life, whatever it may be! . . . How true it is!"

Raskolnikov turns down another street and passes a restaurant, the Palais de Cristal. He goes in, orders tea, and asks the waiter to bring him the newspapers for the last five days. He finds the story about the pawnbroker's murder, reads it, and while he is nervously searching the other papers for later news, Zametov, the head police clerk, sits down beside him.

Zametov, whom Raskolnikov had thought he recognized earlier, has been drinking there with some friends. Raskolnikov makes a deliberate show of saying that he has come specifically to read about the murder. In his choice of words he seems bent on purposely arousing Zametov's suspicions, and at one point uses the words (although mockingly) "I confess." Zametov is completely perplexed. "You are either mad, or. . . ." Then he stopped, "as though stunned by the idea that had suddenly flashed into his mind." "Or what?" demands Raskolnikov. "Nothing," replies Zametov, "it's all nonsense!" Raskolnikov persists in arousing Zametov's suspicions further and, bending close to the police official's face, whispers, "And what if it was I who murdered the old woman and Lizaveta?" Zametov is stunned, but after Raskolnikov leaves he thinks intensely and then decides, "Ilya Petrovitch is a blockhead."

On his way out Raskolnikov bumps into Razumihin, who has been searching for him. Razumihin becomes angry when Raskolnikov makes it clear that he is "sick to death" of him and wants to be left alone, but despite his anger he includes in his shouts at Raskolnikov an invitation to join a party at his apartment that night. Raskolnikov walks onto a bridge, where a woman standing near him suddenly hurls herself into the canal below but is rescued by a policeman. Contemplating this attempted suicide, Raskolnikov murmurs, "that's loathsome . . . water . . . it's not good enough," and turns resolutely toward the police station.

On his way there, however, he passes the old pawnbroker's apartment, is drawn to it again, and enters the building. He arouses the suspicions of some painters who are redecorating the apartment, of the porters below, and of "a man in a long coat." Raskolnikov taunts them as he had Zametov and to their inquiries he replies, "Come to the police station, I'll tell you." Raskolnikov comes to a "cross-roads, and he looked about him, as though expecting from someone a decisive word," but "no sound came." At that moment he sees a crowd gathering around a large carriage down the street, and turns to go there, but not before he makes a firm resolution to go to the police station later, "and it would all soon be over."

Commentary

This chapter brings out fully the conflict in Raskolnikov—whether to live or to die, whether to confess or not, whether to continue in his state of confusion or to accept calmly the consequences that confession would bring.

When Raskolnikov leaves Zametov he hands the waiter "twenty copecks for vodka." This would seem strange, since Raskolnikov had only tea, unless we know that "for vodka" is the equivalent of the French *pourboire,* which means, literally, *for drinking.* It is the phrase used to mean a tip, or gratuity.

QUESTION: After Raskolnikov leaves him, Zametov is "plunged in thought. Raskolnikov had unwittingly worked a revolution in his brain on a certain point and had made up his mind for him conclusively." It is then that Zametov thinks, "Ilya Petrovitch is a blockhead." What do you think Zametov has made up his mind "conclusively" about?

CHAPTER 7

Marmeladov Dies

Summary

Raskolnikov pushes his way through the crowd and sees, lying close to the wheels of a carriage, a bleeding, unconscious man whose face is "crushed, mutilated and disfigured." Apparently, he was drunk and fell under the wheels of a moving vehicle. "I know him!" shouts Raskolnikov. It is Marmeladov.

Raskolnikov directs the police to carry the dying man to Marmeladov's apartment nearby. When they carry in her husband, Katerina Ivanovna, "white and gasping," cries in despair. The three youngest children are terrified. A crowd gathers and the landlady, Madame Lippevechsel, comes up to see what is going on. Marmeladov gasps out, "A priest." A priest and a doctor come but there is no hope, and Marmeladov, knowing these are his last moments, pleads with his eyes for his wife's forgiveness. Sonia has entered "timidly and noiselessly," and under her "rakishly-tilted hat" her eyes stare "in terror." The dying Marmeladov spies her. "Sonia! Daughter! Forgive!" he cries, and dies in her arms.

Raskolnikov thrusts twenty roubles in the hands of Katerina Ivanovna, says he will come again, and leaves. In gratitude, Sonia's half-sister, a child named Polenka, is sent after him by Sonia and her mother. She embraces him warmly. He asks to be included in her prayers, and she declares, "I'll pray for you all the rest of my life." He promises to return the following day.

He walks to the bridge where the woman had tried to drown herself. " 'Enough,' he pronounced resolutely and triumphantly. . . . 'My life has not yet died with that old woman!' " He goes to Razumihin's and finds the party in progress. His friend tells him that Zossimov is becoming increasingly interested in him and thinks that he may be mad. The doctor came to that conclusion, says Razumihin, after Zametov had told them about his conversation with Raskolnikov. They seem no longer to suspect Raskolnikov, but think only that he has somehow become fixed on the idea of the murder during his recent illness. The two men return to Raskolnikov's apartment and are surprised to find his mother and sister, Dounia, waiting.

They greet him joyfully and rush to embrace him. "But he stood like one dead": he cannot move. He tries to walk and falls in a faint. Razumihin takes charge, carries the young man to the sofa, and soon Raskolnikov revives.

Commentary

When Raskolnikov leaves the Marmeladovs' apartment, he is "entirely absorbed in a new overwhelming sensation of life and strength that surged up suddenly within him." Dostoevsky likens this feeling to that experienced by a "man condemned to death who has suddenly been pardoned." Later he cries out "Life is real! Haven't I lived just now?" Raskolnikov is reaffirming life and the will to live.

Katerina calls her landlady by her German name, Amalia Ludwigovna, although the latter insists on being called by her Russian name, Amalia Ivanovna. The landlady is, in fact, German, but resents being called by her German name.

When recalling the past, Katerina Ivanovna thinks of "Prince Schegolskoy, a *kammerjunker*." A *kammerjunker* was a court official similar to a chamberlain.

QUESTION: How would you explain the contrast between Raskolnikov's readiness to give even his last money to the needy and his ability to commit a murder?

PART III • CHAPTER 1
Razumihin Meets Dounia
Summary

The meeting between brother, sister, and mother is a painful one. No sooner does Raskolnikov recover than he tells Avdotya Romanovna (Dounia) that she is to break off with Luzhin: "You are marrying Luzhin for *my* sake. But I won't accept the sacrifice; . . . though I am a scoundrel, I wouldn't own such a sister." And he concludes with, "It's me or Luzhin!" This, of course, greatly upsets both mother and daughter. Although Razumihin has had too much to drink at his house-warming party, his natural vitality and good sense enable him to take charge of this situation. He attributes Raskolnikov's actions to illness, and his impassioned persuasion finally convinces the two women to leave Raskolnikov and go to their lodgings under his escort. He promises to run back immediately to Raskolnikov, bring them news of his condition, then fetch Dr. Zossimov from the party, have him examine the young man, and bring the doctor to them with his report.

Both Raskolnikov's mother and sister are quite impressed with Razumihin. He, on the other hand, has "stared at Avdotya Romanovna without the least regard for good manners." He is very talkative, calls Dounia "angel" and, while walking the women to their room, falls to his knees on the pavement and kisses their hands. In a burst of feeling, he condemns Luzhin as a "scoundrel" for getting them such unsavory lodgings. He is "ridiculous in his sudden drunken infatuation for Avdotya Romanovna. Yet apart from his eccentric condition, many people would have thought it justified." She is a "remarkably good-looking" young woman.

When Razumihin brings Zossimov to the women's lodgings, the

doctor assures them that Raskolnikov will be all right. When the two men are out on the street again, Zossimov comments that Dounia is "a fetching little girl." Razumihin furiously seizes Zossimov's throat and makes it clear to him to leave Dounia alone. He calms down quickly, however, and tells the doctor that he has made arrangements for himself and Zossimov to stay with Raskolnikov's landlady, so that they can keep an eye on Raskolnikov during the night.

Commentary

Dr. Zossimov mentions that Raskolnikov has "something approaching a monomania"—that is, a mental derangement characterized by an irrational preoccupation with one subject—and we learn that Zossimov is "now particularly studying this interesting branch of medicine." This helps to explain much of his interest in and close scrutiny of Raskolnikov.

QUESTION: Why has Razumihin reacted so strongly to Zossimov's comment about Dounia?

CHAPTER 2

Pulcheria Alexandrovna's Dilemma
Summary

It is the next morning. Razumihin wakes up and remembers with disgust how foolishly he spoke and acted with Dounia and her mother the previous evening. He frets considerably, and decides that he has made such a fool of himself that Dounia and her mother can only disdain him. Zossimov enters from the landlady's parlor and he and Razumihin discuss Raskolnikov. Zossimov states that Zametov should not have told everyone at the party the night before about his meeting in the restaurant with Raskolnikov. "But whom did he tell it to? You and me?" says Razumihin. "And Porfiry," Zossimov responds.

Razumihin goes to the lodgings of Raskolnikov's mother and sister, and is delighted to find that he still has their respect. He answers fully their many questions about Raskolnikov and, at their request, gives them a lengthy description of "all the most important facts he knew" of the young man's life during the past three years. He gives a surprisingly objective description of his friend's behavior: "He is morose, . . . proud . . . , suspicious and fanciful. He has a noble nature and a kind heart. He does not like showing his feelings and would rather do a cruel thing than open his heart freely. Sometimes . . . he is . . . cold and inhumanly callous; it's as though he were alternating between two characters."

The discussion then turns to Raskolnikov's desire, about eighteen months previously, to marry his landlady's daughter. No one could understand his attraction to the girl, whom Razumihin describes as "positively ugly," an invalid, and a strange person. It was only her death that prevented the marriage.

Pulcheria Alexandrovna is upset by the details of the meeting between her son and Luzhin, which she asked Razumihin to recount. In this telling, however, he contritely attempts to speak "carefully and even with a certain respect about Pyotr Petrovitch" Luzhin, in contrast to his outburst of the night before, for which he now apologizes. Pulcheria Alexandrovna then shows Razumihin a letter she has just received from Luzhin. In very formal language, Luzhin has stated that he intends to call on the two women that evening but that Raskolnikov must not be present. She cannot decide whether or not to follow Luzhin's instructions and asks for Razumihin's advice. "Act on Avdotya Romanovna's decision," he answers. Her decision is "that Rodya should make a point of being here."

The three of them then leave to visit Raskolnikov, the mother filled with fear of her son who is now so strange. On the way, Pulcheria Alexandrovna tells the others that she dreamed of Marfa Petrovna, and tells Razumihin that she is dead, forgetting he doesn't know who she is. They slowly climb the stairs to Raskolnikov's room, and as they pass the landlady's apartment, they see "two keen black eyes watching them." When their eyes meet, the door is shut with a bang.

Commentary

Raskolnikov's engagement to the landlady's daughter has been mentioned before. Knowing that Raskolnikov can be drawn to such a girl will make his eventual union with Sonia seem quite in character for him and not merely an obvious, contrived plot on the part of the author.

Marfa Petrovna, remember, is the wife of Svidrigailov, who attempted to seduce Dounia while she was employed in their home as a governess.

QUESTION: In the letter that Luzhin wrote to Pulcheria Alexandrovna he states that Raskolnikov gave "twenty-five roubles" to Sonia, whom he characterizes as "a young woman of notorious behaviour." We know, though, that Raskolnikov gave "twenty roubles" to Sonia's *mother* (see Part II, Chapter 7). Why is Luzhin telling this falsehood?

CHAPTER 3

A Strained Meeting
Summary

Zossimov is already at Raskolnikov's when Razumihin and the

mother and sister arrive. "He is well, quite well!" the doctor proclaims. However, it soon becomes apparent that things are not as fine as they seem. Zossimov, for example, notices in Raskolnikov "no joy at the arrival of his mother and sister, but a sort of bitter, hidden determination to bear another hour or two in inevitable torture."

"With all the zest of a young doctor beginning to practice," Zossimov starts to analyze Raskolnikov's present condition, suggesting that work toward a definite goal instead of his present idleness would be most helpful. Raskolnikov agrees: "You are perfectly right. . . . I will make haste and return to the university: and then everything will go smoothly. . . ." But the doctor observes "unmistakable mockery" on his patient's face. As Raskolnikov continues to speak, Dounia sees behind his words and is "intently and uneasily watching her brother."

· Searching for a topic of conversation, Pulcheria Alexandrovna suddenly mentions Marfa Petrovna Svidrigailov's death, which apparently was indirectly a result of the dreadful beatings her husband had lately given her. Raskolnikov speaks of the girl he had intended to marry, saying perhaps it was her constant illness that drew him to her. He then agrees with his mother that his "wretched lodging" has had much to do with his present "melancholy."

Raskolnikov suddenly remembers the "one urgent matter" that has been on his mind, and speaking "gravely" to his sister he says, "If you marry Luzhin, I cease at once to look on you as a sister." Dounia maintains that she is marrying Luzhin not for Raskolnikov's sake, but for her own good. "If I ruin anyone, it is only myself. . . . I am not committing a murder." Her brother pales at the unintended meaning of her words.

Then, trembling, his mother gives him the letter from Luzhin. Before he reads it, Raskolnikov, "as though struck by a new idea," suddenly wonders what he is "making such a fuss for" and tells his sister, "Marry whom you like!" After reading the letter, he makes some very perceptive remarks about the writing style, and is even more convinced that Luzhin is a scoundrel. He labels as "slander" Luzhin's statement that he gave the money to Sonia. Raskolnikov's comment on the letter is: "In all this I see a too hasty desire to slander me and to raise dissension between us." It is agreed, finally, that the four of them, including Razumihin, will meet with Luzhin at the hour he set— eight o'clock that night.

Commentary

At one point in the conversation Raskolnikov attempts to console his mother by saying "Hush, mother. . . . We shall have time to speak freely of everything!" Immediately, however, he is filled with a "deadly chill," for he realizes that "he would never now be able to speak freely of everything—that he would never again be able to *speak* of anything to anyone." Raskolnikov is realizing the full extent of his isolation.

Again we see the extremes in Raskolnikov's nature as he fluctuates from one moment to the next in his attitude toward Dounia's marriage to Luzhin.

QUESTION: When Zossimov advises Raskolnikov to avoid the "fundamental causes" that brought on his illness and suggests a method by which he might achieve complete recovery, Raskolnikov agrees with him, but with derision. What ironic meaning in Zossimov's words could have produced such "mockery" in Raskolnikov?

CHAPTER 4

Several Meetings
Summary

Just then the door opens and Sonia enters, "overwhelmed with shyness, like a little child." Raskolnikov introduces her to his family. Sonia has come to invite Raskolnikov to her father's funeral and to the "funeral lunch," which will take place the next day. Her shyness and "kindliness" win over the other two women, so that "there was a light in Dounia's eyes, and even Pulcheria Alexandrovna looked kindly at Sonia." After asking Raskolnikov and Razumihin (with a special entreaty from Dounia) to dinner, Raskolnikov's mother and sister leave, and Raskolnikov turns back to Sonia, "looking brightly at her."

After a while, Raskolnikov tells Razumihin that he had recently pawned a ring and a watch with the murdered pawnbroker. Since Porfiry Petrovitch has been "inquiring for people who had pawned things," he asks his friend if it might be advisable to see Porfiry about it personally. "The matter might be settled more quickly." "Let us go at once," Razumihin replies.

Sonia, too, leaves, wanting to "meditate on every word, every detail" of her meeting with Raskolnikov, for "dimly and unconsciously a whole new world was opening before her." Lost in thought, she does not see the fashionably dressed man, "about fifty," who had begun following her in front of Raskolnikov's house. This same man had been passing by as she was taking leave of Raskolnikov and Razumihin, and on hearing her words "he turned a rapid but attentive look upon all three." "I've seen [her] face somewhere," he had thought, and he had decided to follow her home. When she reaches her apartment at Kapernaumov's the tailor, he stops at the apartment next door and, laughing, says, "How odd! . . . We are neighbours."

Meanwhile, Raskolnikov and Razumihin have proceeded to Porfiry's. Raskolnikov is alert, his mind works rapidly, and he begins to calculate how much Porfiry may actually know about him. He carefully plans just the right appearance he must present, and then, "with a sly smile," he begins to tease Razumihin about his apparent infatuation with Dounia. This seemingly innocent jesting provokes a good deal of laughter as they enter the passage to Porfiry's apartment. "This is what Raskolnikov wanted: from within they could be heard laughing as they came in."

Commentary

A sudden and drastic change has come over Raskolnikov. His confusion has turned to cunning, and his incoherence has given way to a remarkable clarity. At the moment when he is finally to face the police (as represented by Porfiry), all possibility of confession has been abandoned. His only thought now is to outwit Porfiry.

The stranger who follows Sonia home wonders at "the strange coincidence" that they should be neighbors: again we see the element of chance entering into Dostoevsky's novel.

QUESTION: Why has Raskolnikov decided to go see the head of the Investigation Department?

CHAPTER 5

Raskolnikov Meets Porfiry
Summary

Raskolnikov and Razumihin enter Porfiry's apartment. Raskolnikov, on his guard, weighs every word, every gesture, and craftily calculates his every move so as not to arouse Porfiry's suspicions. The chief detective greets them gaily, reflecting their mirthful mood. He is about 35, "short, stout," and with a face that would have been "good-natured" except for a look in his eyes that reveals "something far more serious than could be guessed at first sight." Zametov, who has "been sitting in the corner," rose smiling to greet them, and his "unexpected presence struck Raskolnikov unpleasantly."

When Raskolnikov mentions the watch and ring, Porfiry says that they were labelled with his name so there is no danger of their being lost but, if the student desires, he may write a brief note formally requesting that his property be held until he can redeem it.

The young student at first seems to carry off the conversation successfully. Nothing that Porfiry says to him seems amiss, yet the *way* he says things and the *way* he looks at Raskolnikov makes the student think to himself, "He knows." He increasingly becomes convinced that Porfiry and Zametov suspect him and that they are only playing cat-and-mouse with him. But, "What if it's only my fancy?" he asks himself.

Porfiry turns the conversation to an article that Porfiry has read, written by Raskolnikov and published two months before, without the author's knowledge, in a periodical. The article analyzes "the psychology of a criminal before and after the crime" and describes Raskolnikov's theory of the "extraordinary man"—a type of man who has the right to commit a crime and set himself above the law. Raskolnikov explains and defends his theory at length. Porfiry suggests directly that perhaps Raskolnikov considers himself an "extraordinary man" and even perhaps a man able to "rob and murder." "If I did I certainly should not tell you," answers Raskolnikov.

Before Raskolnikov leaves, Porfiry says that instead of writing that note he may come to see him personally, adding that he will be at the police station at 11 o'clock the next day. Then Porfiry asks Raskolnikov whether he saw two painters when he went up to the old woman's apartment. Raskolnikov answers cautiously and is suddenly interrupted by Razumihin, who shouts, "What do you mean? Why, it was on the day of the murder the painters were at work, and he was there three days before? What are you asking?" Porfiry excuses himself for having been confused on the point, and, in an overly polite way, sees them to the door.

Commentary

At the beginning of the chapter, the reader is certain (or almost certain) that Raskolnikov has successfully fooled Porfiry by "*assuming* a serious air," by giving the "*appearance* of most genuine fun, and by being able to "*feign* embarrassment." And yet, at the first touch of irony in Porfiry's words, we know, or can guess, that Porfiry isn't being fooled one bit and, in fact, is capable of matching Raskolnikov at his own game.

Raskolnikov explains his "extraordinary man" theory in the following way. Mankind is divided into "ordinary" people, who live according to the law and exist only to reproduce the human race, and "extraordinary" people, who may break laws in order to advance humanity and bring it a "new word." The "extraordinary man" does not have the right to break laws at random but may break them if, "in his own conscience," it is necessary to do so in order to bring mankind a "new word." As an example, Raskolnikov maintains that "if the discoveries of Kepler or Newton" could be made known only by "sacrificing" lesser people, then these men would have had the right to "eliminate" those others. He maintains that most of the "benefactors and leaders of humanity were guilty of terrible carnage," mentioning the lives lost by those defending the old order against the one these "great men" sought to establish. We will learn later that Raskolnikov considers Napoleon the supreme example of the "extraordinary man."

Several words in this chapter may need to be explained.

A *phalanstery* is a socialist community or community building of the type established according to the principles of Charles Fourier (1772-1837), the French social philosopher. The word *phalanstery* is derived from the Greek word *phalanx*, which referred to a closely ranked body of troops. In the Fourierist meaning, a *phalanx* was an economic rather than a military unit, made up of 1,620 persons, who lived in a *phalanstery*.

New Jerusalem is "the Heavenly City" mentioned in the Bible, Revelation 2:21.

Lazarus is another Biblical reference. It alludes to the miracle performed by Jesus when he raised Lazarus from the dead. Porfiry asks Raskolnikov whether he believes in this miracle literally, and the young man says he does. And, to the extent that he begins a new moral and spiritual life, Raskolnikov experiences a similar miracle.

A *retort* in chemistry is a curved glass vessel in which substances are distilled by heat. When asked to explain a fine point of his "extraordinary man" theory, Raskolnikov replies, "I have not peeped into the retort in which all this takes place."

QUESTION: What evidence, if any, do you think Porfiry has against Raskolnikov?

CHAPTER 6

Raskolnikov Dreams of the Murder
Summary

As Raskolnikov and Razumihin walk away from Porfiry's apartment, Razumihin is excited. He thinks it unforgivable that Porfiry could suspect a person who has been as ill as Raskolnikov. Suddenly an "alarming idea" occurs to Raskolnikov, and he abruptly leaves Razumihin.

Raskolnikov hurries home to examine the hole in his apartment wall, for he had suddenly had the uneasy thought that, by accident, he had left some piece of evidence there that would be found. The hole is empty, however, and he leaves his apartment. As he goes through the gateway he becomes aware that the porter is pointing him out to a man "wearing a long coat" who has been asking about him. Raskolnikov follows the man for a long while, and when he overtakes him and asks, "Why do you . . . come and ask for me . . . and say nothing," the man utters one word: "Murderer!" Raskolnikov is shaken and returns to his room "feeling chilled all over." He lies down and, when Razumihin and Nastasya open the door looking for him, he pretends to be sleeping. He thinks many tormenting thoughts, torturing himself and realizing that he has debased his theory with this bungled crime. He then falls asleep and dreams.

In his dream, Raskolnikov again sees the man in the long coat, who beckons to him. He follows him up the stairs of a house and then realizes it is the place where the old pawnbroker lived. He enters her apartment, takes up his axe, and strikes her again and again, but she only laughs, "shaking with noiseless laughter." He tries to run away but the halls and stairs are full of people. Raskolnikov wakes and sees sitting beside him a strange man who says, "Arkady Ivanovitch Svidrigailov, allow me to introduce myself. . . ."

Commentary

One of the thoughts that occurs to Raskolnikov is that he should "have known beforehand" that he would be unable to live with a calm conscience after he had "shed blood." He is not, after all, an "extraordinary man." He is not like the "real *Master*" who could massacre cities and abandon armies without a thought. (Raskolnikov is referring to Napoleon.) On the contrary, he now considers himself an "aesthetic louse," for he carried out the murder not as a means toward a "grand and noble object" (as an "extraordinary man" would), but "for my own fleshly lusts."

Raskolnikov also thinks, "I didn't kill a human being, but a principle." He is not very concerned with the life he took, but feels angry that the pawnbroker was not a worthy enough subject to test his theory. "I shall never, never forgive the old woman!" he thinks.

Raskolnikov has hardly given a second thought to his murder of Lizaveta. Her murder was unimportant in terms of his theory, yet he realizes that he "scarcely ever" thinks of her, "as though I hadn't killed her." Thoughts of Lizaveta make him think, too, of Sonia, both "poor gentle things, with gentle eyes. . . . Why don't they moan?" This is somewhat reminiscent of his dream about the poor gentle mare who was beaten about the eyes and died without uttering a sound. Again his dual nature is clear: he feels sympathetic and tender toward "poor gentle things"—and yet he murdered one.

At one point, Razumihin refers to the temperature in the police station as being "thirty degrees Reaumur." The French physicist, René Antoine Ferchault de Reaumur (1683-1757), invented a temperature scale in which the freezing point of water is 0° and the boiling point is 80°. Thirty degrees Reaumur equals 100° Fahrenheit.

QUESTION: Raskolnikov ponders the problem of the identity of the man in the long coat, and we might ask as he does: "Who is he?"

PART IV • CHAPTER 1

Enter Svidrigailov
Summary

Raskolnikov looks "suspiciously" at Svidrigailov, who explains that he has come to ask the young student's help in a matter regarding Dounia. Before he reveals what it is, the two men talk: Svidrigailov in a somewhat flattering, amused way, and Raskolnikov in a generally hostile manner. They talk about Svidrigailov's past relationship with Dounia, which he explains by saying that he is human and "capable of being attracted and falling in love," and was simply a victim of his emotion. Raskolnikov says that Svidrigailov has "got rid" of Marfa Petrovna, his wife, to which the older man replies that his conscience is clear—he beat her very lightly. His wife's ghost, he continues, has appeared to him three times since she died, and each time talks of the silliest trifles. "What made me think that something of the sort must be happening to you?" says Raskolnikov suddenly. Svidrigailov is astonished, but replies, "What! . . . Didn't I say that there was something in common between us?"

Their talk continues about ghosts and the afterlife. Then Raskolnikov wants to know why Svidrigailov has visited him. Svidrigailov explains that as part of his "necessary preliminary arrangements" for a "certain . . . journey," he wants to see Dounia, "if you like in your presence," to apologize for his past actions toward her and to give her a gift of ten thousand roubles so that she can break off with Luzhin. He insists that his proposal has no ulterior motive. Raskolnikov refuses the offer and Svidrigailov replies, "I shall be obliged to try and see her myself." At any rate, adds Svidrigailov, "Marfa Petrovna remembered her in her will and left her three thousand roubles." As he leaves, he meets Razumihin entering the room.

Commentary

Despite Raskolnikov's feeling of repulsion toward Svidrigailov, an odd attraction exists between the two men. At the moment it is more apparent to Svidrigailov, who calls the two of them "birds of a feather." One point of similarity is that Svidrigailov is thought to have contributed to the death of two people (his wife and a servant, Philip) and has been haunted by their ghosts; Raskolnikov has killed two people and is haunted by one of them in his dreams.

At one point in the conversation, Svidrigailov refers vaguely to a "journey," and when Raskolnikov later inquires when it will begin, Svidrigailov replies, "If only you knew what you are asking." This is the first intimation of Svidrigailov's suicide.

Svidrigailov states to Raskolnikov that "I, too, am a man *et nihil humanum . . . .*" This Latin phrase is derived from a statement by the second century (B.C.) Roman playwright, Terence, that *"Humanus sum et nihil humanum alienanum puto"* ("I am a human being, and I consider no thing human alien to me").

Three French phrases also appear in this chapter: *bonne guerre* (in the sense of "good move"); *j'ai le vin mauvais* ("I am sad in my cups," or, an idiomatic equivalent, "I cry in my beer"); and *pour vous plaire* ("to please you").

Svidrigailov refers to a document his wife gave him on his "name day." A name day is the feast day of the saint after whom a person is named, and is often observed in addition to, or instead of, the person's birthday.

QUESTION: What do you think of Svidrigailov, in the light of the foregoing comments?

CHAPTER 2

The Meeting
Summary

Raskolnikov and Razumihin hurry to the eight o'clock appointment with Dounia, her mother, and Luzhin. Raskolnikov tells his friend about Svidrigailov and says they must guard Dounia from him, to which Razumihin enthusiastically agrees. He then informs Raskolnikov that he visited Porfiry and Zametov to try to chastise them for insulting Raskolnikov with insinuations about the murder, but he "couldn't speak in the right way." For the first time, Raskolnikov wonders what his friend's reaction will be when he learns the truth.

When they arrive at the women's lodgings, they all sit down "at the round table where a samovar was boiling." The conversation begins with some minor exchanges between Luzhin and the two women; then "all was silent." When Pulcheria Alexandrovna mentions that Marfa Petrovna has died, Luzhin says that Svidrigailov has arrived in Petersburg. He calls Svidrigailov "depraved" and "abjectly vicious" and accuses him of an act of "fantastic and homicidal brutality" against a young girl some years before. His final story is about Philip, one of Svidrigailov's servants, who, Luzhin claims, Svidrigailov drove to suicide. Dounia doubts the truth of these stories and says, "When I was there [as a governess] he behaved well to the servants, and they were actually fond of him."

Raskolnikov astounds the others by revealing that Svidrigailov has just been to see him and that Dounia has been left three thousand roubles by Marfa Petrovna. Luzhin is very upset when Raskolnikov adds that Svidrigailov has an offer, which he doesn't reveal, to make to Dounia. The conversation becomes more earnest, and Dounia says that the time has come for her to make a choice between Luzhin and her brother. Luzhin is terribly offended at being set "on a level with an impertinent boy." This in turn infuriates Dounia, and as she responds to Luzhin he becomes even more pompous and puffed up with self-importance. Their bitterness increases until Dounia, "white with

41

anger," says, "Pyotr Petrovitch, go away." Luzhin "turned pale," unable to believe that he has lost Dounia. He loses control of himself, saying that he should not have been so generous as to ignore the "universal verdict" about her character after the incident in Svidrigailov's home, and to offer to marry her as a means of "reinstating her reputation." As he leaves, Luzhin "carried away in his heart . . . vindictive hatred . . . against Raskolnikov" but did not entirely abandon the hope that all would "be set right again."

Commentary

Here we see the contrasting sides of Svidrigailov's character, as Luzhin relates stories of his past and Dounia recalls him as a well-liked master of his servants. If we believe Luzhin's stories, then Svidrigailov is indeed evil. Raskolnikov senses the dark side of Svidrigailov, telling Razumihin on the way to the meeting, "He is very strange, and is determined on doing something."

A samovar is a Russian urn for making tea.

QUESTION: Do you think that Dounia's attitude toward Luzhin might have been different if she had not been told about the three-thousand-rouble legacy from Marfa Petrovna?

CHAPTER 3

Raskolnikov Leaves His Family
Summary

Luzhin is quite put out at this recent turn of events. For many years Luzhin has laid his plans to marry a poor, virtuous, beautiful, well-educated, timid girl who would "look on him as her saviour," and feels that he cannot live without Dounia, who fills all the specifications so perfectly. Resolving to settle everything on "the very next day," he imagines that he can handle the brother and his friend— the only one he really fears is Svidrigailov.

Meanwhile, Raskolnikov's mother, Dounia, and Razumihin are very "relieved," although Raskolnikov is "almost sullen and indifferent." He tells the whole story of Svidrigailov's visit and Dounia, almost shuddering, says, "He has got some terrible plan."

Razumihin outlines his idea to borrow money from his uncle and, with the Raskolnikovs contributing a similar amount from Dounia's money, they can all go into partnership in a book publishing venture. The two women are enchanted with the idea, but at the peak of their enthusiasm Raskolnikov, preparing to leave them, stutters that they should "forget" him, and then "slowly went out of the room."

Razumihin overtakes him in the hallway. It is dark. They stand near a lamp, "looking at one another in silence. Razumihin remembered that minute all his life." Raskolnikov's eyes meet his friend's, "piercing into his soul, into his consciousness." Razumihin starts. "Something strange . . . passed between them. . . . Some idea, some hint . . . slipped, something awful, hideous, and suddenly understood on both sides." Razumihin turns white as a sheet. He understands everything.

"Go back, go to them," Raskolnikov says and, turning suddenly away, leaves the house. Razumihin returns to Dounia and her mother, and "from that evening Razumihin took his place with them as a son and a brother."

Commentary

The experiences that bind together Dounia, her mother, and Razumihin in this chapter contrast sharply with Raskolnikov's actions. Gaining the promise of money, parting with the obnoxious Luzhin, and facing the possibility of a bright future together, so meaningful to the three, are nothing more than shadows to Raskolnikov. His quiet departure just at this moment points up his utter isolation and the depth of his decision to work out his fate entirely alone. He says to his family, "Whatever may come to me, whether I come to ruin or not, I want to be alone."

QUESTION: What is it that Razumihin understands?

CHAPTER 4

Raskolnikov and Sonia
Summary

Raskolnikov goes directly to the house where Sonia lives. When she sees him, she feels "sick and ashamed and happy, too." They talk about Katerina Ivanovna and her children and, when Sonia speaks, "a sort of *insatiable* compassion . . . was reflected in every feature of her face." Raskolnikov says that her mother will "soon die," and he utters the words coldly and without pity. He continues "with a harsh smile" that Sonia's fate will also befall Polenka, her young sister. "No, no! God will protect her, God!" she cries. " 'But, perhaps, there is no God at all,' Raskolnikov answered with a sort of malignance, laughed and looked at her." She cannot speak and begins sobbing bitterly. Raskolnikov paces silently about the room. He comes to her, looks into her face, and, "dropping to the ground, kissed her foot." He did it, he tells her, as a tribute to "all the suffering of humanity."

Raskolnikov is struck by a nagging thought: what keeps her from suicide, insanity, or complete depravity? "So you pray to God a great deal, Sonia?" he asks. "What should I be without God?" she replies. He thinks, "That's the way out! That's the explanation." He picks up a Bible that lies on her bureau and asks her where she got it. Upon learning it is from Lizaveta, he thinks " 'Strange!' . . . Everything about Sonia seemed to him stranger and more wonderful every moment." Suddenly he asks her to read the passage about Lazarus, whom Christ raised from the dead. She falters in her reading, and he suddenly realizes that this is her *"secret treasure,"* it is what has sustained her in all her suffering, and now she wants to read it to him and have *him* believe as she believes. She reads about Lazarus with "intense emotion"; it is "the story of the greatest miracle and a feeling of immense triumph came over her." The end of a sputtering candle flickers over "the murderer and the harlot who had so strangely been reading together the eternal book." Raskolnikov tells her he has parted with his family and admits, "I need you, that is why I have come to you." About to leave, he says, "If I come to-morrow, I'll tell you who killed Lizaveta." He leaves, and throughout the night Sonia is "feverish and delirious."

Soon after Raskolnikov leaves, a man walks on tiptoe out of the vacant room adjoining Sonia's where he had been at the door, listening to the entire conversation. He goes to his own room and returns with a chair that he places beside the door, so that on the next day he can listen in greater comfort. The man is Svidrigailov.

Commentary

Raskolnikov mercilessly suggests to Sonia all the horrible possibilities that might befall the persons she loves. This is not characteristic of Raskolnikov, and we must look for his motive. It is supplied later in the chapter when he tells Sonia "I have chosen you out. . . . I chose you out long ago to hear this [who killed Lizaveta]." Raskolnikov wants to be absolutely certain that Sonia will be able to accept his revelation, not because he is afraid she will inform on him but because he wants someone he can share his burden with, someone who is able to bear extreme horror. After he has tested her, he kisses her foot, explaining that she epitomizes human suffering. A moment later he again refers to her "great suffering." We shall see by the end of the novel that the theme of suffering has achieved a central importance in the book.

Although he rejects everyone else, Raskolnikov is able to accept Sonia, and in accepting her he breaks the bonds of his isolation. The relationship between Raskolnikov and Sonia develops into the principal relationship in the book. Note also that their coming together occurs during a reading of the Lazarus story, symbolic of Raskolnikov's eventual rebirth.

QUESTION: Why does Svidrigailov take such an interest in Raskolnikov's conversations with Sonia?

CHAPTER 5

Raskolnikov Calls on Porfiry

Summary

The next morning, promptly at 11 o'clock, Raskolnikov goes to the police station to see Porfiry about the pawned watch. "He had expected that they would pounce on him" and is surprised to find that he is not being guarded. After ten minutes, when he is admitted to Porfiry's office, Raskolnikov notes "signs of certain awkwardness" in the chief detective.

They engage in what seems to be a superficial conversation, but again, as before, Raskolnikov sees double meanings everywhere.

After numerous hints by Porfiry, Raskolnikov replies that he is now aware that Porfiry suspects him of the double murder. As "his eyes glowed with fury" he demands a formal accusation, if that is what Porfiry intends. Porfiry tells the young man that he knows he went to the pawnbroker's apartment and "rang the bell and asked about the blood." But then, disclaiming any ulterior motives, he becomes solicitous about Raskolnikov's well-being. "I have a sincere liking for you and genuinely wish you good," he says. Raskolnikov rises to go and demands to know whether he is perfectly free from any suspicion. "And won't you see my little surprise?" Porfiry asks. "My little surprise, it's sitting there behind the door, he-he-he! . . . I locked him in that he should not escape." Suddenly, from behind a second door, people are heard approaching, and something completely unexpected by either occurs.

Commentary

Porfiry states that he sincerely wishes Raskolnikov "good," and earlier he has said a somewhat cryptic "I tell you these things for nothing and don't even expect a reward for it." This would seem to explain why Porfiry withdraws from a direct accusation. Porfiry seems to have something in mind other than merely apprehending Raskolnikov.

At one point, Porfiry states that had he chosen the military as his field "I shouldn't have been a Napoleon, but I might have been a major." This ironic reference is to Raskolnikov's former allusion to Napoleon as the supreme example of the "extraordinary man."

Raskolnikov calls Porfiry a "punchinello," that is, a buffoon like Punch, who is traditionally a squat, grotesque person. The insult carries double weight in view of Porfiry's own short and stout appearance.

Again we encounter some foreign phrases: *tout court* ("merely"); *c'est de rigueur* ("it is according to strict etiquette"); and the "Austrian *Hof-kriegsrat*" (the Austrian War Council).

CHAPTER 6
An Unexpected Event
Summary

To Porfiry's dismay, several persons thrust themselves into the room. At the fore is Nikolay (the arrested painter), who kneels before Porfiry and proclaims, "I am the murderer." Porfiry, confounded, clears everyone out of the room and dismisses Raskolnikov, who says, "I believe we can say *good-bye*!" "That's in God's hands," responds Porfiry, but he adds that they *will* meet again as he must still ask the young student some questions.

Raskolnikov returns home, where he reflects on these recent events. He feels temporarily out of danger but knows for a certainty that Porfiry is "bound to win." But when he goes to open the door to leave for Marmeladov's "memorial dinner," it opens by itself—the mysterious stranger in the long coat appears, bows very low, and apologizes to Raskolnikov. It is he who has gone to the police and told them that Raskolnikov had visited the pawnbroker's apartment after the murder and had invited everyone to follow him to the police station. The man says he had told Porfiry about it moments before Raskolnikov entered the police station, and apparently it was *he* who was the "surprise" waiting behind the closed door! After the man leaves, Raskolnikov determines to "make a fight for it."

Commentary

Had Raskolnikov determined only to "fight for it" this chapter would have ended merely on a note of melodrama. However, Dostoevsky's closing description raises this chapter (as numerous other instances elevate the entire novel) to the realm of great psychological drama.

QUESTION: Why has Nikolay said that he is the murderer?

PART V • CHAPTER 1

Luzhin Begins a Plot
Summary

On the same morning that Raskolnikov is with Porfiry at the police station, Pyotr Petrovitch Luzhin is fretting over his recent rejection by Dounia. The information that Raskolnikov will be among those at Marmeladov's funeral dinner "suggested an idea" to him and, "somewhat thoughtful," he enters the room he is sharing with Andrey Semyonovitch Lebeziatnikov.

Andrey Semyonovitch, who had once been Luzhin's ward, is "an anemic, scrofulous little man" who has "attached himself to the cause of progress," for he is one of those who follow "the idea most in fashion only to vulgarize it." Luzhin seeks his company in order to learn which doctrines are in favor among the younger generation in Petersburg. However, Luzhin has discovered that he has not picked a good source of information—Lebeziatnikov has no important connections and picks "things up third-hand."

As Luzhin sits down to count some bundles of money, he asks Lebeziatnikov whether the latter is friendly enough with Sonia to ask her in. Lebeziatnikov says yes, and fetches Sonia from the dinner (his apartment is in the same house). Luzhin seats her facing him over the table full of money, and suggests to the shy, embarrassed girl that a fund be started for Katerina Ivanovna. He gives Sonia a ten-rouble note as the first contribution, with the stipulation that his name not be associated with his gift.

When Sonia departs, Lebeziatnikov turns to Luzhin and praises him for the generous act he has just witnessed, saying, "I heard and *saw* everything." He gives the sentence an unusual emphasis. Luzhin will have none of the praise, however, and terms it "nonsense." Luzhin "was preoccupied with something else, . . . seemed excited and rubbed his hands. Lebeziatnikov remembered all this and reflected upon it afterwards."

Commentary

Dostoevsky's portrait of Lebeziatnikov as a ridiculous, naïve radical is indicative of the author's attitude toward the young progressives of his time, with whom he had been much involved when he himself was young.

Luzhin counts his money with a "reckoning frame"—an abacus. Invented in ancient times, the abacus is still used in parts of Russia today.

The French word *distinguons* means, "Let us make the distinction." It is used by Lebeziatnikov in differentiating between the role of the prostitute in the present and in the future society.

QUESTION: What "idea" do you think suggested itself to Luzhin near the start of the chapter and is now preoccupying his mind? Could it be related to whatever it was that Lebeziatnikov *"saw"*?

CHAPTER 2

The Funeral Dinner
Summary

Katerina Ivanovna wants to show the other lodgers that she knows "how to entertain," and payment for the dinner has consumed "nearly ten of the twenty roubles" given to her by Raskolnikov. Most of the lodgers have stayed away, however, and the dinner party is made up only of "wretched creatures": an "unfortunate little Pole," who had helped run errands while preparations were being made; two of the Pole's friends, whom no one has ever seen before; an old, feeble man; a drunken retired clerk; one or two others; and the landlady, Amalia Ivanovna, whose obvious pride in having prepared the table and the food (while the widow was at the cemetery) infuriates Katerina Ivanovna. In anticipation of a large turnout, the children have been given their food at a makeshift table in a corner.

Raskolnikov, too, comes. Katerina is incensed at the gathering before her, and tells Raskolnikov, in loud whispers punctuated with severe coughing, that it is all the fault of "that cuckoo," Amalia Ivanovna. Sonia arrives late from her meeting with Luzhin. Loudly enough so that everyone can hear, because she knows it will gratify her mother, she tells her that Luzhin will be over as soon as possible "to discuss *business* alone with her and to consider what could be done for her." The message has the anticipated effect on Katerina Ivanovna.

Everything goes terribly. The few guests get drunk, make ribald fun, and try to jeer Katerina into a fight with the German landlady, who she feels "must be responsible for those who were absent." Katerina begins to openly insult the landlady, making fun of her faulty Russian, as "the flush on her cheeks grew more and more marked." After further insults the landlady can stand no more. She shrieks and runs about the room, shouting threats. When she refers to Sonia as "the yellow ticket," Katerina runs at her. Suddenly, Luzhin enters the room and looks sternly at all present. Katerina rushes to him.

Commentary

Various foreign words appear in this chapter: the Pole calls Katerina Ivanovna *pani,* which is Polish for "Mrs.," and she in turn once calls him *pan,* or "Mister." Amalia Ivanovna refers to her *Vater aus Berlin,* or "father in Berlin" who was a *burgomeister,* which is an office equivalent to that of mayor. She also mentions *die Wäsche,* or "the laundry." Her certificate of honor contains a statement about her father *en toutes lettres,* or "at full length, unmistakably."

QUESTION: Why has Luzhin decided to come to the dinner after all? Might there be some connection with his "idea"?

CHAPTER 3

Luzhin Interrupts the Dinner
Summary

When Katerina Ivanovna flees to Luzhin for protection, he coldly waves her off. It is Sofya he wants to see, he says, using Sonia's formal name. Behind him Lebeziatnikov soon appears and stands, "perplexed," in the doorway. Then Luzhin accuses Sonia of taking a hundred-rouble note from the table in his room during her visit. He magnanimously adds that if she will reveal the location of the money, "the matter shall end there." Otherwise, he will have to resort to "very serious measures." Sonia denies any knowledge of the theft. Luzhin then gives a pompous, detailed account of how and why he obtained the money and of the meeting between Sonia and himself. Terror-stricken, Sonia whispers, "I have taken nothing," and offers the ten-rouble note to Luzhin. He refuses it.

The landlady leads the guests in accusing Sonia of the theft. Katerina Ivanovna takes the ten-rouble note and flings it "straight into Luzhin's face." Eager to demonstrate her daughter's innocence, she screams, "Search her!" She turns Sonia's pockets inside out, and suddenly a small folded piece of paper flutters to the floor at Luzhin's feet. Luzhin stoops, picks it up, and holds it before the dinner guests. It is the money. Amalia Ivanovna is in a frenzy at this discovery of a "thief" and orders the family to move out. Katerina is in utter despair, her "tears unrestrained as a child's" as she clasps her daughter in her wasted arms, crying that Sonia is capable of nothing but self-sacrifice—"she sold herself for us!"—and calling for someone to defend her. Those present cannot help being moved. Even Luzhin feels *"compassion"* and grandly declares he "will carry the matter no further."

"How vile!" comes a voice from the doorway. It is Lebeziat-nikov. He angrily denounces Luzhin for having put the hundred-rouble note in Sonia's pocket himself while shaking hands with her before she left. He cannot explain why Luzhin tried to make her appear a thief. It is obvious that the guests have changed their opinion and now believe Sonia innocent. Luzhin attempts to defend himself and to discredit Lebeziatnikov.

Raskolnikov, all the while silent, says, "I can explain why he risked such an action." He tells the audience of the recent affair between Luzhin and his family. He concludes that Luzhin has attempted to discredit Sonia in order to prove to Dounia and her mother that Luzhin's insinuations about Sonia in his letter were correct. This would have alienated Raskolnikov from them and again established Luzhin as Dounia's fiancé. "Everyone was crowding around Luzhin with threats and shouts of abuse," and Lebeziatnikov orders him to move out of his lodgings. Luzhin leaves with a show of insolence and the announcement, "I shall prosecute." As he leaves, a glass hurled at him mistakenly hits Amalia Ivanovna. She becomes enraged and, blaming Katerina Ivanovna for all the unpleasantness, she begins to throw the widow's belongings on the floor and orders her out of the apartment. Katerina, half mad, rushes at her, but the landlady is too strong, and the deathly ill woman runs out of the apartment to find "justice." Sonia, overcome at last by the utter helplessness of her position in the world, had left minutes before, and now Raskolnikov, too, leaves, "in the direction of Sonia's lodgings."

Commentary

Notice that Luzhin, wishing to call Sonia by her formal name, gets the middle name wrong. Her name is Sofya Semyonovna; Katerina's middle name is Ivanovna.

At one point, Amalia Ivanovna shouts, *"Gott der Barmherzige!"* or "God the merciful!" The three Poles repeatedly shout at Luzhin, "The *pan* is a *lajdak!*" or "The man is a good-for-nothing!"

QUESTION: The last half-dozen chapters cover a very brief time. About two-thirds of the novel is now over. What would you say is the total time that has elapsed?

CHAPTER 4

Raskolnikov Confesses to Sonia
Summary

It is a little while later. Raskolnikov has arrived at Sonia's apartment. He pauses at the door, unable to summon the courage to tell her who killed Lizaveta, yet knowing he *must* do so without delay. When he tells her that her mother ran off "to seek justice," she wants to run after her, but Raskolnikov prevents her, saying, "Stay a little with me." Reminding her how close she came to being imprisoned because of Luzhin, thus bringing on the ruin of her mother and the children, he poses a question to her: If she had to choose, would she decide that the evil Luzhin should live and consequently Katerina Ivanovna would die, or that Luzhin should die so that her mother might live? Sonia insists that her opinion would never play a part in such a decision—these things are left to the Divine Providence.

He turns the conversation back to the murder. When Sonia asks him how he knows about *"it,"* he replies, with a "distorted, helpless smile," "Guess." When she says she cannot guess, he tells her, "Take a good look." As she realizes the meaning of his words, he sees in her face the same terror that filled Lizaveta's face when he raised the axe. He begins to feel that terror himself. After the first moment of speechless horror, she takes him in her arms. "There is no one—no one in the whole world now so unhappy as you!" she cries, weeping hysterically. She promises to follow him to Siberia, but he "recoiled," and with a "hostile, almost haughty smile," said, "Perhaps I don't want to go to Siberia yet, Sonia."

When Sonia asks him why he committed the crime, Raskolnikov is unable to explain it to her or to himself. He suggests it was for the money, or because he wanted to be a "Napoleon," but rejects those reasons. He rejects too that it was because the pawnbroker was only a "louse." But then, feverish, he says, "He who dares most of all will be most in the right! . . . I wanted *to have the daring* . . . and I killed her. . . . I wanted to find out . . . whether I can step over barriers, . . . whether I am a trembling creature or whether I have the *right*. . . ."

After rejecting all the reasons he has suggested for his crime, Raskolnikov says, "I want to prove one thing only, that the devil led me on then and he has shown me since that I had not the right; . . . I am just such a louse as all the rest. . . . I murdered myself, not her! . . . it was the devil that killed that old woman, not I." Suddenly, with a face filled with despair, he asks, "Well, what am I to do now?"

Sonia replies, "Go at once, this very minute, stand at the crossroads, bow down, first kiss the earth which you have defiled and then bow down to all the world and say to all men aloud, 'I am a murderer!' Then God will send you life again." He refuses to give himself up, however, saying they would laugh at him for killing her and then not being able to take the money, but hiding it under a stone instead. "I'll make another fight for it," he states with a "haughty smile." Raskolnikov then tells her that the police are after him and that perhaps he will be jailed temporarily. When Sonia says that she will visit him he "felt how great was her love for him," but "strange to say he felt it suddenly burdensome and painful to be so loved." He asks her not to see him in prison; she does not answer, she is crying. She offers him her cross of "cypress wood." At first he says, "Give it to me," but then he declines it, saying, "Better later." She agrees, saying she will put it on him "when you go to meet your suffering; . . . we will pray and go together."

They hear a familiar voice at the door, and Lebeziatnikov appears.

Commentary

Sonia's advice to go to the crossroads and confess seems to hearken back to Part II, Chapter 6, when Raskolnikov stood at the crossroads "as though expecting from someone a decisive word. But no sound came." Sonia expresses Dostoevsky's belief that suffering leads to salvation, and that suffering begins only after confession. Raskolnikov, however, is not yet ready to confess and take up this burden; therefore, he is not ready to accept Sonia's cross, the symbol of suffering.

Here, too, we see Sonia's own deep capacity for bearing severe trials. In addition to all she has endured in life, she is able to share Raskolnikov's heavy affliction, not only for the moment but until that distant time when his suffering will end.

In this chapter we see the reason for Raskolnikov's continuing downfall. He is unable to abandon his intellectual conviction that he may be *right*—that as a completely free individual he can "step over barriers" without being punished. Opposed to that conviction is the belief, upheld by Sonia, that man is a child of God and has a moral nature that cannot be violated with impunity. Raskolnikov must first acknowledge that man's nature is fundamentally moral and confess his wrongdoing; only then can he begin the path of regeneration toward salvation.

In his search to find the reason for his crime, Raskolnikov mentions for the first time a possible "tendency to insanity." There have been several references to his "monomania," and many of his symptoms are characteristic of schizophrenia, which is a type of mental disease characterized by loss of contact with one's environment and by disintegration or splitting of personality. Recall that in Part III, Chapter 2, Razumihin says of Raskolnikov, "It's as though he were alternating between two characters."

QUESTION: Why has Lebeziatnikov come?

CHAPTER 5

Katerina Ivanovna Dies
Summary

Lebeziatnikov tells Sonia and Raskolnikov that Katerina Ivanovna is acting as though she has lost her mind. She has gone out on the street with the children and is making them sing and dance for money. Sonia rushes out.

Raskolnikov walks back to his room. "Never, never had he felt himself so fearfully alone!" He regrets that he has divulged his secret to Sonia and poisoned her life, and resolves, "I will remain alone and she shall not come to the prison!" He is struck with the idea that it might actually be better in Siberia. At that moment Dounia enters.

Dounia says that Razumihin has told her *"all"*—that the reason Raskolnikov is so upset is that the police suspect him of a murder. She tells him to call on her, if he needs "all my life or anything." As she leaves, he praises Razumihin and says good-bye to her in a way that makes her ask, "Are we really parting for ever that you . . . give me such a parting message?" When she is gone, he reflects that he wanted to hug her, "even to *tell* her," but he felt that "afterwards she may shudder when she remembers that I embraced her. . . . And he thought of Sonia."

Although he does not realize it, he is very ill. Nevertheless, he goes out, and soon Lebeziatnikov catches up with him and says that he and Sonia have found Katerina Ivanovna and the children. He leads Raskolnikov to where they are, at a place by the canal right next to Sonia's lodgings. Katerina Ivanovna's "wasted consumptive face looked more suffering than ever," and she acts madly, screaming at the children to sing and dance the verses and steps she has taught them. A crowd has gathered around them to laugh and jeer. She urges Polenka to speak the French she has taught her, to show that they are "of good family, well brought-up children." The crowd and the disturbance draw a policeman, and at his approach the two younger children flee in terror. Katerina Ivanovna runs after them, "weeping and panting for breath," stumbles, and falls. Blood rushes from her lungs. She is carried to Sonia's room where, in a last flow of memories, songs, and soft words for Sonia, Katerina Ivanovna dies.

"Sonia fell upon her, flung her arms about her, and remained motionless. . . . Polenka threw herself at her mother's feet, kissing them and weeping violently." Svidrigailov, who had entered the room earlier, now draws Raskolnikov to one side. He says that he will provide financially for the three children and put them in "some good orphan asylum" and also provide for Sonia. In his conversation, Svidrigailov, with "sort of a gay winking slyness," uses words and phrases that Raskolnikov had used the evening before when confessing to Sonia. " 'How do you know?' Raskolnikov whispered, hardly able to breathe." Svidrigailov, laughing, explains that he lives next door. "I told you we should become friends," he says.

Commentary

Raskolnikov wants to tell his sister the truth but doubts that she could "stand that test" as Sonia had. Prior to this feeling of wanting to confess he considers "Siberia" as "better" than the life he is enduring at the moment. Despite his vehement refusal to consider imprisonment in Siberia when Sonia had suggested it on their previous meeting, now, for the first time, he considers it as a possibility. His manner of saying good-bye to Dounia also indicates that Raskolnikov is slowly turning round in his mind the final steps toward confession.

Among the foreign words and phrases found in this chapter are: *tenez-vous droite!* ("stand up straight!"); *parlez-moi français* ("speak French to me"); *Glissez, glissez, pas de basque* ("Glide, glide, the basque step"); *Du hast Diamanten und Perlen* ("You have diamonds and pearls"), *Du hast die schönsten Augen* ("You have the loveliest eyes"), *Mädchen, was willst du mehr?* ("Maiden, what more do you want?"). The last three lines are from a song that Dostoevsky heard at his sister's home while he was working on this fifth part of the book. It was a melody often played by Moscow organ-grinders.

QUESTION: What are your feelings about Katerina Ivanovna? How does she illustrate the theme of "suffering" that has been mentioned throughout the book?

PART VI • CHAPTER 1

Raskolnikov and Razumihin Part

Summary

An uneasy period begins for Raskolnikov, one filled with "dreary solitude" and fears. Svidrigailov is one of his chief worries, although in encounters with Svidrigailov there has been no direct mention of the confession the older man overheard. Only once, when they meet on the stairs in Sonia's building, does Svidrigailov say there are "things they must talk over." He suddenly asks Raskolnikov why he looks so upset, adding, "what all men need is fresh air . . . more than anything!"

After this encounter, Raskolnikov stands at the door of Sonia's room, where a requiem service is being sung over the body of Katerina Ivanovna. "By Svidrigailov's orders it was sung twice a day punctually." At the end of the service Sonia takes both Raskolnikov's hands in hers and puts her head on his shoulder. This puzzles Raskolnikov, who detects "no trace of repugnance, no trace of disgust, no tremor in her hand."

During this same period Raskolnikov frequently takes long walks, "but the lonelier the place was the more he seemed to be aware of an uneasy presence near him." Once, when he is in a tavern listening to the singing—and enjoying it—he suddenly feels uneasy, "as though his conscience smote him." But instantly, as if he is again putting up his guard, he thinks, "No, better the struggle again! Better Porfiry again . . . or Svidrigailov . . . ."

He wakes the next afternoon at two o'clock. He remembers that it is the day of Katerina's funeral and is glad that he is missing it. Razumihin enters, evidently greatly disturbed about something. He says he has come only "to find out once for all whether it's a fact that you are mad," adding that many people think this is the case. He criticizes Raskolnikov for ignoring Dounia and his mother, who is now very ill. After talking to Raskolnikov, Razumihin decides, "Above all, you are not mad." As Razumihin starts to leave, Raskolnikov says that he is "going in for a drinking bout," and stops him by saying that he spoke with Dounia about him. Razumihin becomes "drunk without wine" when he hears that Dounia may love him.

When Raskolnikov mentions that he is going to see a man who told him that "what a man needs is fresh air" and find out what he meant, Razumihin concludes that he is a "political conspirator . . . on the eve of some desperate step." He thinks Dounia is in on this plot, and that an upsetting letter she has just received is connected with it. He is puzzled to find that Raskolnikov did not know about the letter. As he is once more about to leave, Razumihin remembers the news that Nikolay, the painter, "has confessed and given the proofs" of his guilt in the pawnbroker's murder—Porfiry himself gave Razumihin the psychological "explanation of it." Razumihin finally leaves, cursing himself for having suspected, as the result of their encounter "under the lamp in the corridor that day," that his friend is the murderer.

Raskolnikov does not believe that Porfiry sincerely accepts Nikolay's confession and wonders why the chief detective has not contacted him for so long. Raskolnikov feels that he must see Svidrigailov and then Porfiry, but as soon as he leaves his room he bumps into Porfiry in the hallway. " 'You didn't expect a visitor, Rodion Romanovitch,' Porfiry explained, laughing." Raskolnikov feels no fear, only a kind of relief, at seeing him. The two men sit down in Raskolnikov's room, facing each other.

Commentary

When Raskolnikov says, "Better the struggle again!" we may ask "better" than what? This is a further indication that his thinking has been turning more and more toward confession. At the end of his "uneasy period," Raskolnikov seems ready for some resolution, no matter what it may be. When Porfiry appears, Raskolnikov is "scarcely afraid of him" and even thinks to himself, "Perhaps this will mean the end."

QUESTION: Why has Porfiry visited Raskolnikov?

CHAPTER 2

Porfiry Accuses Raskolnikov
Summary

After making small talk about his smoking habit, Porfiry announces, "I've come to have it out with you." For the first time, Raskolnikov sees "a touch of sadness" in Porfiry's face. The chief detective reviews all that has happened since the murder, revealing how the police "purposely spread rumours" that Raskolnikov was guilty to anger Razumihin and, through him, to "excite" Raskolnikov. He then goes on to a discussion of Nikolay, immediately admitting he did not believe his confession, "not for a minute"—he had told Razumihin that he did believe it just to calm the young man down. Nikolay, he explains, is a fervent member of a religious sect and he confessed so that he might "take his suffering," since suffering for its own sake is a vital aspect of his religious beliefs.

"Then . . . who then . . . is the murderer?" asks Raskolnikov breathlessly. Porfiry seems "amazed at the question."

" 'Why, *you*, Rodion Romanovitch! You are the murderer,' he added, almost in a whisper, in a voice of genuine conviction."

At first Raskolnikov denies it, "like a frightened child caught in the act," but then asks Porfiry why he came—"If you consider me guilty, why don't you take me to prison?"

Porfiry replies that he is presenting Raskolnikov with the opportunity to "surrender and confess," thereby earning a lighter sentence and making the detective's job much easier.

Raskolnikov raises the possibility that Porfiry may be mistaken in his accusation, but the latter says that he has "a little fact," that he will not reveal, to prove Raskolnikov's guilt. Suddenly, the young man shouts that he does not care about shortening his sentence. Porfiry tells him not to give up on life, that "this may be God's means for bringing you to Him. . . . You are not hopelessly base." He explains that Raskolnikov has needed "a change of air" for a long time and that suffering "is a great thing." And he feels that even if Raskolnikov went to prison without having confessed, he would, in a few months, confess of his own volition "and perhaps to your own surprise."

They both rise to leave. Raskolnikov reminds Porfiry that he has confessed nothing. In a roundabout way, Porfiry requests that if Raskolnikov should decide to commit suicide ("an absurd proposition") he leave a note indicating that he is the murderer and mentioning the stone—"It will be more generous." Porfiry leaves, and a few minutes later Raskolnikov, too, "went hurriedly out of the room."

Commentary

In Chapter 1 of Part VI, Raskolnikov felt that the "end" was near. We see the degree to which he is ready to accept his fate when, in this chapter, "the thought that Porfiry believed him to be innocent began to make him uneasy."

Note how the "suffering" theme is again elaborated upon in this chapter, this time by Porfiry.

Porfiry's offer to delay Raskolnikov's arrest for a day or two and give him an opportunity to turn himself in has a two-fold purpose. On the superficial level it will enable Raskolnikov to get a lighter sentence. More important, however, Porfiry realizes that voluntary confession is essential, for it could be the first step toward regeneration.

Porfiry's remark, "It will be more generous," apparently refers to Nikolay, and the fact that a note of confession would clear the innocent painter of suspicion.

Foreign words: *umsonst*, in vain; *Morgenfrüh*, tomorrow morning.

QUESTION: When Raskolnikov asks Porfiry if he may be "mistaken" in his belief that he, Raskolnikov, is guilty, the detective replies that he has "a little fact" that he will not divulge. We interpret this to mean that Porfiry has a bit of irrefutable evidence. What could it be?

CHAPTER 3

Svidrigailov and Raskolnikov Meet Again
Summary

When Raskolnikov leaves his room he goes directly to Svidrigailov's. He cannot understand why he is "hastening to Svidrigailov"—they can certainly have nothing in common. "Their very evil-doing could not be of the same kind." He feels very strongly that the man has plans to use the confession he overheard "as a weapon against Dounia."

He stops in the street to see where he is, and finds himself near a tavern. Suddenly, in one of the windows, he spies Svidrigailov, who obviously does "not want to be seen." When he realizes that Raskolnikov has noticed him, he invites him in. The tavern is filthy, "not even second-rate." Svidrigailov is in a private room, and dismisses the young boy and girl who were playing and singing for him.

After several minutes of conversation, Raskolnikov comes "straight to the point," telling Svidrigailov that if he does attempt to take advantage of Dounia, "I will kill you. . . . You can reckon on my word. You know I can keep it." Svidrigailov calmly implies that this is all in Raskolnikov's imagination. He also says that he is "just going off somewhere" and can spend only a hour with Raskolnikov. He begins chatting about himself and his passion for women. Without this, he says, he might become so bored "I might have to shoot myself." When Raskolnikov asks if he could do it, Svidrigailov's face changes and he replies, "Please don't speak of it"—he is "afraid of death" and dislikes talking of it. He continues chatting and suddenly, Raskolnikov, feeling "oppressed and stifled," begins to leave. Svidrigailov begs him to remain a while longer, and promises to tell him about a woman who once tried to "save" him. The woman is Dounia.

Commentary

At the very beginning of this chapter, Raskolnikov thinks that Svidrigailov has "some hidden power over him," and that "he had long felt that he must see him for some reason." He seems puzzled by Svidrigailov's conflicting character, which alternates between generosity and selfishness. Perhaps, at first, Raskolnikov thinks that Svidrigailov might be an "extraordinary man." Raskolnikov discovers another answer, however, for at the moment he rises to leave "he felt convinced that Svidrigailov was the most worthless scoundrel on the face of the earth."

QUESTION: Svidrigailov mentions to Raskolnikov that he is soon going "somewhere," and, later, he says that "there's a certain fact that has wound me up tremendously." What do you think is on his mind?

CHAPTER 4

Svidrigailov's Story
Summary
Svidrigailov talks first about his wife, Marfa Petrovna. He then begins discussing Dounia, saying that at first he had entirely avoided her, but that after his wife had told Dounia all the "gossip" about him, Dounia had sought him out to try and save him. Driven by desire for her, he offered her all his money—thirty thousand roubles—to run away with him to Petersburg. "But it ended in the catastrophe of which you know already."

Raskolnikov insists that the older man still has evil designs on Dounia, and Svidrigailov retorts, "That's all nonsense!" He is, he explains, "betrothed" to a girl not yet sixteen, "a charmer" whose parents approve of the match for financial reasons. Svidrigailov continues talking, telling what Raskolnikov calls "nasty anecdotes," until the young man cries, "Enough!" and accuses him of being a "depraved, vile, sensual man."

The two men soon leave, Svidrigailov "preoccupied with something of importance." Raskolnikov has become very suspicious of him and decides to follow him.

Commentary
When Svidrigailov says that he is engaged to such a young girl Raskolnikov says that he "understands" now why the other has provided for Sonia and her younger brother and sisters. He suspects that evil intentions underlie this act of seeming generosity, just as he suspects that Svidrigailov still may have designs on his sister.

Foreign words and phrases: *oraison funèbre,* funeral oration; *cher ami,* dear friend; *la nature et la vérité,* nature and truth; *cancan,* a kind of dance; *vis-à-vis,* face to face; *la vertu va-t-elle se nicher?* who could expect to find virtue there?; *assez causé,* enough!; *adieu, mon plaisir,* goodbye, my joy.

QUESTION: Do you feel that the "something of importance" bothering Svidrigailov is about to occur?

CHAPTER 5

Svidrigailov Faces Dounia
Summary
As the two men leave the tavern Raskolnikov tells Svidrigailov, "I am not going to lose sight of you now" for, he explains, "I am positive

that you have not given up your designs on my sister." Svidrigailov threatens to call the police, but when Raskolnikov remains undaunted, the older man turns jocular and says he is only going to his apartment for money.

They go to Svidrigailov's apartment, he takes some money, and then he hails a cab and gets in. "Raskolnikov decided that his suspicions were at least for that moment unjust." He walks away. If he had looked back, he would have seen Svidrigailov "get out not a hundred paces off, dismiss the cab and walk along the pavement." Raskolnikov sinks, "as usual, into deep thought." He stands on the bridge, gazing at the water. He is not aware that he passed Dounia a moment before and that she is now standing beside him. She does not know whether to speak. Suddenly, she sees Svidrigailov beckoning her and she goes up to him.

It is apparent from their conversation that he sent her the disturbing letter and that this meeting was mentioned in it. Dounia wants to talk there in the street, but Svidrigailov persuades her to come to his apartment. He says it is likely that Sonia is at home, and gives the impression that there are many other people living on his floor.

Once upstairs, Svidrigailov points out that the empty rooms adjoining his apartment also adjoin Sonia's, and he shows Dounia the chair he sat on while listening to the conversation between Sonia and Raskolnikov. They sit down at opposite ends of a table and Svidrigailov relates what he overheard her brother confess. At first, Dounia refuses to believe him, but slowly she accepts it as true. When she asks about the reasons for the crime, Svidrigailov recounts briefly her brother's theory about superior beings. Dounia tells him she read of the theory in an article Razumihin brought to her. She expresses a wish to see Sonia, and he says that she will not be back until late.

"Ah, then you are lying!" She runs to go out and find Raskolnikov, but the door is locked. Svidrigailov insists she sit down and talk it over. She asks, "How can you save him?" and Svidrigailov answers, "It all depends on you, on you, on you alone." He then professes his love for her, but this only frightens Dounia. She shakes the door, crying, "Open it!" Svidrigailov tells her that he has lost the key and that no one can hear her. Dounia draws a revolver from her pocket.

Svidrigailov is completely surprised, but almost his first words are, "You've made things wonderfully easier for me." She calls him a murderer, saying she knows he poisoned Marfa Petrovna. "Even if that were true," he replies, "it would have been for your sake." Moments later he "took a step forward and a shot rang out. The bullet grazed his hair. . . . 'Fire again, I'll wait,' " Svidrigailov says, and reminds her that she must cock the revolver.

Again he steps toward her and again she pulls the trigger, but it doesn't fire. Now but "two paces away," Dounia aims a third time, but "suddenly she flung away the revolver." Svidrigailov feels delivered, not from death but "from another feeling, darker and more bitter." He tries to embrace Dounia but she repulses him. "There followed a moment of terrible, dumb struggle in the heart of Svidrigailov." He suddenly turns away from her, places the key on the table and, with a terrible urgency, orders Dounia to leave—"Make haste!" When she has gone, "a strange smile contorted his face, a pitiful, sad, weak smile, a smile of despair." Thoughtfully, he picks up the revolver and leaves.

Commentary

Svidrigailov has brought Dounia to his apartment not merely to force himself upon her. He wants to marry her, and promises to be her "slave" forever. He even offers to take her and her family out of the country. The extent of his feeling toward Dounia is shown after she throws away the gun and Svidrigailov feels himself delivered from a "feeling, darker and more bitter" than death itself. He has interpreted this action as a sign of caring, perhaps even of some love, for him, and he embraces her. It is then that he is unequivocally repulsed by Dounia, has a moment of "struggle" in his heart, and moves away from her. He is not interested in possessing Dounia physically, but needs her to want him emotionally. His great plan a failure, he lets Dounia go.

Svidrigailov uses the French phrase *une théorie comme une autre,* which means "one theory is like another."

QUESTION: Remember that Raskolnikov had wondered how his sister would have stood the "test" of knowing the truth about him. How do you think Dounia's attitude toward her brother, now that she knows he is a murderer, will compare with Sonia's?

CHAPTER 6

Svidrigailov's Final Act
Summary

When Svidrigailov leaves his room he wanders "from one low haunt to another" until 10 o'clock that evening. It begins to rain, and Svidrigailov returns home. He takes all his money, visits Sonia, and gives her bonds valued at three thousand roubles. "I may be going to America," he says, adding that now she can change her way of living. She tries to refuse the money, but he explains that Raskolnikov "has two alternatives: a bullet in the brain or Siberia." When Sonia looks startled, he assures her that he will tell no one, but that if Raskolnikov goes to Siberia, "you will follow him. That's so, isn't it? And if so, you'll need money. You'll need it for him." When he leaves Sonia is filled with "vague apprehension."

He then calls on his betrothed, giving her fifteen thousand roubles and telling her family that business calls him away from the city. At midnight he crosses the Little Neva, gazing at the water with "special interest," and searches for a particular hotel he remembers. He finds it, and is given a small cubicle of a room under the stairway. The rain, the wind, and the cold have made him feverish. Annoyed, he thinks, "It would have been better to be well for the occasion." He wraps up in a blanket and lies down.

Finally, he drowses and seems to feel mice running all over his body under the bedclothes. He starts to chase them and wakes up. He tries not to think, but dozes again. He imagines that it is Trinity day, and he is in a house bedecked with fragrant flowers. In the middle of the drawing room, in a white coffin, is a young girl whom Svidrigailov knew. Only fourteen, she had drowned herself because someone had "smirched that angel purity . . . on a dark night in the cold and wet."

He imagines that he is again awake and gets out of bed. He hears a clock strike three and thinks, "It will be light in an hour? Why wait?" He hurries out to find the "ragged attendant," pay for his room, and leave. Suddenly, in a dark corner by a cupboard he notices a little girl of about five, crying and shivering, her clothes soaking wet. He takes her to his room and wraps her in his warm blanket. He starts to leave, but then returns to see if the little girl has fallen asleep. As he gazes at the child, her face is transformed into "the shameless face of a French harlot." He raises his hand to strike her, but awakes.

Fully awake, he dresses and, taking a notebook from his pocket, writes "a few lines in large letters" in a conspicuous place. After a while he walks "resolutely" from his room and out of the hotel. He comes to a large house where a man, dressed as a kind of guard, leans against the gates. Svidrigailov says that he is going "to America" and, as the man's eyes grow "bigger and bigger" and he protests, "This is not the place for such jokes!" Svidrigailov places the revolver against his head and pulls the trigger.

Commentary

Part of the enigma surrounding Svidrigailov has been peeled away. At least one of the rumors about him, the one that hinted he was the cause of a young girl's death, is revealed as true in Dostoevsky's description of Svidrigailov's dream and thoughts afterward.

The dream about the little girl that fills him with such horror is a further indication of Svidrigailov's base character. But his reaction in the dream shows that he is still capable of despising, though not controlling, this sensuality in himself.

Svidrigailov mentions a *café chantant*. This is a French term for a tavern where music is provided. He also goes to a "pleasure garden" that is described as a "Vauxhall." The name is apparently derived from Vauxhall Gardens, for many years a popular London pleasure area. Vauxhall Gardens was closed down in 1859, just a few years before *Crime and Punishment* was published.

QUESTION: Do you think that Dostoevsky's use of dreams is effective?

CHAPTER 7

Raskolnikov's Final Decision

Summary

On the evening of the day Svidrigailov kills himself, Raskolnikov "had reached a decision." He goes to his mother's apartment and finds her there alone. She weeps with joy at seeing him and promises not to question him about his activities. They talk for a while, and his mother mentions that Dounia "seems to have got some secrets of late" and has been out a great deal.

Suddenly, Raskolnikov says, "Please listen to me. . . . I've come to assure you that I've always loved you. . . . Though you will be unhappy, you must believe that your son loves you now more than himself." Pulcheria Alexandrovna embraces him and says that she has known for a long time that there is "a great sorrow in store" for him. He admits he is going away, tells her she cannot come with him, and asks her to "kneel down and pray to God for me. Your prayer perhaps will reach Him." She blesses him with the sign of the cross, and he falls down before her, kissing her feet and weeping. "For the first time after all those awful months his heart was softened." She does not want him to leave, but he tears himself away, asking her to pray for him and promising to "come to-morrow."

He returns to his room and finds Dounia waiting for him there. He looks at her, "and from those eyes alone he saw at once that she knew." Then Raskolnikov asks whether, knowing what she does, she can still offer him her hand. At these words she embraces him, and suggests that by deciding to give himself up and face his suffering he is "half expiating" his crime.

In a "sudden fury" he cries, "What crime?" He asserts that killing "a vile noxious insect" like the old pawnbroker "was atonement for forty sins." He is giving himself up, he says, only because "I am contemptible and have nothing in me. . . . If I had succeeded I should have been crowned with glory, but now I'm trapped. . . . I fail to understand why bombarding people by regular siege is more honourable." With rising feeling he concludes, "I am further than ever from seeing what I did was a crime."

The anguish he sees in Dounia's eyes stops him, and he says that the time has come for him to go "somewhere else." He asks her to stay with their mother, and promises to be "honest and manly all my life, even if I am a murderer." Suddenly his thoughts turn to his impending punishment, and he cries, "What's the object of these senseless sufferings? Shall I know any better what they are for, when I am . . . weak as an old man after twenty years' penal servitude?"

Finally, the brother and sister leave the apartment and go their separate ways. Dounia turns around to look at Raskolnikov again; he, too, turns "and for the last time their eyes met." But an angry gesture tells her to leave him, and a moment later he repents the gesture. "Oh, if only I were alone and no one loved me and I too had never loved anyone! *Nothing of all this would have happened.*"

He walks through the streets, hating the people around him ("every one of them a scoundrel and a criminal at heart and, worse still, an idiot") and wondering for "the hundredth time" in twenty-four hours *why* he is going to confess—"but still he went."

Commentary

The focal point of this chapter is Raskolnikov's persistent inability to view the murders as a crime. He feels that if he is guilty of anything, it is of failing to prove his theory and for that alone he is "contemptible." He also fails to understand that suffering can lead to expiation and regeneration—to a new life—as his sister suggests to him. He flings it all back into her face, as he has done before to other people. Then why is he still going to confess? Perhaps to *end* the suffering he has been enduring. As he himself says, "perhaps too for my advantage, as that . . . Porfiry . . . suggested!"

QUESTION: Can you think of any other reason why Raskolnikov has decided to give himself up?

CHAPTER 8

Raskolnikov Confesses
Summary

Raskolnikov goes to Sonia. Dounia had been there, and she and Sonia, in their mutual love and concern for Raskolnikov, had become close friends. Dounia had left comforted by the knowledge "that her brother would not be alone." Raskolnikov enters the room. "I have come for your cross," he tells her, but she guesses from the way he says them that "the words were a mask." Sonia takes two crosses out of a drawer. Making the sign of the cross over herself and Raskolnikov, she places the wooden one around his neck, the other, of copper, around her own.

Raskolnikov mocks the situation—" 'It's the symbol of my taking up the cross,' he laughed. 'As though I had not suffered much till now!' " He tells Sonia that she will have her wish—he is going to prison. He gets angry when she begins to weep, "but his feeling was stirred; his heart ached, as he looked at her." He cannot say what he really wants to say, so he crosses himself and starts to leave. Realizing that Sonia intends to go with him, he tells her sharply that he will go alone, and leaves without even saying good-bye. Out on the street he asks himself why he has come to see her, and believes that he wanted only to "see her terror" and have "something to delay" him. He walks out of his way to mingle with the crowds. Suddenly, he recalls Sonia's words, "Go to the cross-roads, bow down to the people, kiss the earth, . . . and say aloud to the whole world, 'I am a murderer.' " This memory overwhelms him—"everything in him softened at once and the tears started into his eyes. He fell to the earth on the spot."

He kneels "in the middle of the square" and kisses the earth "with bliss and rapture." Once again he does it. His actions elicit sarcastic comments from people nearby, and their laughter stifles whatever intention he may have had of confessing aloud as Sonia had suggested. Sonia herself, Raskolnikov has noticed, is standing not far off, watching him. "Raskolnikov at that moment felt and knew once for all that Sonia was with him for ever and would follow him to the ends of the earth, wherever fate might take him."

He goes to the police office, mounts the stairs, and enters. Ilya Petrovitch appears from another room and greets him. Then Raskolnikov inquires after Zametov and learns he had left the day before after arguing with everyone. This leads Ilya Petrovitch to a new topic of conversation, and he chats merrily on. His talk turns to suicides, and he mentions the most recent—Svidrigailov. This startles Raskolnikov, who turns pale, says, "I must go" and, after a most cordial farewell from the lieutenant, stumbles giddily down the stairs. Outside, he sees Sonia, "horror-stricken. . . . He stood still before her. There was a look of poignant agony, of despair, in her face." He manages a smile, and goes back upstairs.

When he tries to speak to Ilya Petrovitch, nothing but "incoherent sounds" result. The lieutenant has him sit down and shouts for some water. Raskolnikov waves the water aside, "and softly and brokenly, but distinctly said: *'It was I killed the old pawnbroker woman and her sister Lizaveta with an axe and robbed them.'* "

Commentary

Ilya Petrovitch says of Raskolnikov that "all the attractions of life *nihil est.*" This is to say that all such attractions *are nothing* to Raskolnikov.

Ilya Petrovitch inquires whether Raskolnikov is a Nihilist. A Nihilist was a member of a particular Russian political party that advocated extreme revolutionary reforms and often resorted to terrorism. He also asks Raskolnikov whether he has read "Livingstone's Travels." This is a reference to the book *Missionary*

Travels written by the famous Scottish missionary and explorer David Livingstone and published in 1857.

The contents of the final message that Svidrigailov wrote in his notebook are revealed. Its purpose was apparently to make sure that no one is blamed for his death but himself. This provides one more insight into the man's character—he knew what was "right" and in this case was able to do it.

QUESTION: When Raskolnikov overhears that Svidrigailov has killed himself it is "as though something has fallen on him and was stifling him." Dostoevsky does not explain why Raskolnikov feels this way. What reason would you give?

EPILOGUE • PART I

Summary

It is Siberia, almost a year and a half after the murders. Raskolnikov has stood trial and has been in prison for nine months.

Mainly because it was felt he had committed the crime "through temporary mental derangement" and because he made no attempt to defend himself, his sentence was "penal servitude . . . for a term of eight years only."

Two months after he and Sonia (who had followed him as all had understood she would) left for Siberia, his sister and Razumihin were married. Pulcheria Alexandrovna had developed a "strange nervous" illness during the trial, and a few weeks after the marriage she died.

Meanwhile, in the town near Raskolnikov's prison, Sonia has established herself as a seamstress and her quiet efficiency has drawn people to her. Raskolnikov, withdrawing from everyone, became very ill and was admitted to the prison hospital.

PART II

Summary

"He was ill a long time." But it was not prison life that had done it—"it was wounded pride that made him ill." If only he could feel that he was wrong to have murdered, if only he could suffer the agonies that a repentant conscience would bring—then he might find relief.

Raskolnikov gets out of the hospital after Easter, and recalls the strange dreams he had while ill. He dreamed that the world was swept by a mysterious plague that was going to destroy all but a chosen few. Those attacked by the plague considered their own ideas to be infallible and, as a result, men, communities, and nations destroyed each other in the belief that they alone possessed the truth. Devastation was everywhere. But, strangely, the "pure chosen ones" were nowhere to be found. The memory of this dream haunts him for a long time.

Soon after the dream, Raskolnikov learns that Sonia is sick. He misses her, and when he receives a note from her saying she is better "his heart throbbed painfully." One "warm bright day" soon after, Raskolnikov is sent to work with two other prisoners along the river. The guard and the other prisoners are some distance away, and he suddenly "found Sonia beside him; she had come up noiselessly and sat down at his side." Then "all at once something seemed to seize him and fling him at her feet. He wept and threw his arms round her knees." Sonia, in turn, understands that "at last the moment had come." Without a word, they know that "the heart of each held infinite sources of life for the heart of the other." In spite of the seven years' imprisonment that lies ahead, "he had risen again and he knew it."

That night, it seems to him that everything has changed! At last, "life had stepped into the place of theory and something quite different would work itself out in his mind." He reaches under his pillow, and there, lying untouched, is the New Testament from which Sonia had read to him the story of the raising of Lazarus. He opens it.

Commentary

Dostoevsky's use of the words "repentance," "resurrection," and "he had risen again" to describe Raskolnikov's final transformation are evidence of the theme of Christian belief that runs throughout the novel. Notice that Raskolnikov's illness does not end until after Easter, and it is shortly after his recovery that he experiences his spiritual rebirth. Easter, of course, is the one holiday in the Christian calendar that commemorates a "rebirth"—the rising of Christ.

The dream Raskolnikov has in prison is the turning point of his spiritual struggle. Until then, he is unable to admit the wrongness of his crime and suffers from extreme pride, but following the dream he is filled with the repentance that begins his regeneration. The dream reveals the horrible nature of his theory. Carried to its conclusion, with everyone acting only according to his own beliefs, his theory would lead to a world of anarchy, chaos, and complete destruction. The utter emptiness of the theory is exposed, and the last shred of pride dissolved, when the few chosen ones who were to be saved to begin "a new race and a new life" are nowhere to be found.

Character Sketches

Raskolnikov

Raskolnikov is an intelligent young man caught between circumstances beyond his control and a plan of cold-blooded murder that he himself devises and rationalizes. The tension, in Raskolnikov, between a desire for perfect control over emotions and circumstances that threaten to betray him, is extreme. In fact, his mind is a strange blend of reason and madness. He writes a paper justifying atrocities done by titanic geniuses; then, after a hallucinatory dream in which a man kills his helpless mare, Raskolnikov coolly slays an old woman and her sister.

Raskolnikov is without a moral anchor. Dounia, his sister, and Sonia, the daughter of his misguided friend Marmeladov, come closest to bringing out the humanity in him. But his attitude toward the law and toward humanity is supremely detached. Not even his attempts at faith are convincing. And his apparent generosity in giving money away freely cloaks his inability to sympathize. He lives in a sea of people yet is alienated from mankind. The murders in part explain why he is cut off, but perhaps they are an excuse too. Even when he has planned to be most in control of destiny, he gets more than he bargained for — Lizaveta's death was not in the plan.

Svidrigailov

Svidrigailov is in some ways a "double" for Raskolnikov. He is implicated in crimes — the deaths of his wife Marfa and of Resslich's niece. He exhibits apparent generosity in his offer to help Marmeladov's orphaned children. He labors against a world from which he has become separated. Where Raskolnikov has a dream before killing Alyona and Lizaveta, Svidrigailov has a dream before his suicide. He senses a special kinship between himself and Raskolnikov. Yet he is quite different from Raskolnikov. He is more sophisticated, more in control, more cynical about man's possibilities. He is lascivious, and he has money. Unlike Raskolnikov, he never seems to affirm man's possibilities. Even though much of his evil reputation is founded on rumor, he seems even more lost than Raskolnikov.

Marmeladov

Marmeladov despairs of making anything of himself. When he gets a chance to pull himself and his family out of degradation, he purposely destroys it and himself. He is full of self-pity, but he lacks the will to confront his own evil. His death under the carriage wheel is symbolic — he has been crushed by the wheel of fortune that is life.

Yet he has caused his sensitive daughter's fall to sin and causes his wife's madness and his children's ruin. His language is full of religious allusions, but he has no religion. He likes to confess everything — but without conviction or contrition.

Porfiry Petrovitch

Porfiry Petrovitch outsmarts Raskolnikov by guessing that he is the murderer. He is not only extremely rational; he is a master of human psychology. The first time Raskolnikov dares to insinuate to Petrovitch that he, Raskolnikov, is guilty, the police investigator speaks of the ability of some people to convince themselves that they have done what they have not. And when he finally accuses Raskolnikov of the crime, he does so on the basis of intuition, not hard evidence. He must rely on Raskolnikov's admission for conclusive proof. In one sense, Petrovitch exemplifies the need for both the orderly presentation of evidence and for psychology to triumph over logic. It would be an exaggeration to say that Petrovitch is the one humanitarian in the novel. Rather, he takes a genuine interest in the workings of the criminal mind.

Sonia

Sonia, the young prostitute who has turned to religion and who becomes Raskolnikov's confidant and bridge to life, is almost saintly. She is forced to sin to get money for her mother, siblings and drunken father. Frail and sensitive, she takes responsibility for others without hesitation. She is genuinely religious, and ironically she has gained in her faith from contact with Lizaveta Ivanovna, whom Raskolnikov kills. It is not clear how she will ultimately affect her beloved in Siberia and afterward. Her willingness to make the sacrifice is in keeping with her character, but it is not done out of weakness of will or despair.

Dounia

Dounia, Raskolnikov's sister, is, as he himself realizes, like Sonia in many ways. She proposes to sacrifice her own happiness to marry Luzhin in order to gain the money with which Raskolnikov can continue his studies. To her brother this selling of herself is like Sonia's prostitution, and he wants the match to be broken off. Dounia, however, is not like Sonia in any material respect. She leaves Svidrigailov's service in disgrace because she is falsely accused of having slept with him. Later, she is vindicated by Marfa, his wife. Dounia never allows Luzhin to get close and finally breaks with him. And she rebuffs Svidrigailov even when her brother's crime is used against her. She has her brother's sense of personal integrity, but chiefly for that reason she is inadequate to assist him in his development. She is much more vivid as a character than Sonia because she is more self-possessed and less perfect. She is also less deep. Incapable of the suffering of Sonia, she is nevertheless still admirable, and psychologically makes a good match for Razumihin, who is attracted to her.

Lizaveta Ivanovna

Lizaveta Ivanovna, unlike her sister Alyona Ivanovna, has character, but it is discovered only after she has been senselessly slaughtered by Raskolnikov. At first she seems to be wholly overshadowed by her sister. She is dominated and appears weak-willed. Yet through Sonia she is charitable, genuinely Christian, and even pathetic. Lizaveta has given Sonia access to a religion that complements her inner nature.

Razumihin

Razumihin, Raskolnikov's friend, takes a genuine concern in Raskolnikov's condition; but in spite of his otherwise close relationship he cannot share Raskolnikov's terrible secret of murder. He is quick and intelligent, helpful and hospitable. But he is incapable of the fine appreciation of the human psyche that would reveal to him what his friend cannot disclose. He is not a Petrovitch. His ability to relate to his sometimes delirious friend parallels that of Dounia, for whom he has considerable affection. He loves life and cannot understand Raskolnikov's problems.

Luzhin

Luzhin is unworthy of Dounia. All he has going for him is his money, and he is quite conscious that he is "buying into" the Raskolnikov family. Whereas Svidrigailov represents the depravity of the leisured class, Luzhin represents its banality. While he is not the immoral and affected type that Lebeziatnikov is, he is a bore lacking intelligence and feeling.

Pulcheria

Pulcheria, like her son, is a victim of circumstances that have brought her low. She wants the best for her son, and even encourages her daughter to seek a match that will bring the means for Raskolnikov's continued education. Yet her mind is so fixed on her own comfort and the external aspects of her son's education, that she cannot recognize Raskolnikov's real needs and thoughts.

Literary Elements

Plot

The outline of Dostoevsky's plot is fairly straightforward. Raskolnikov plans to kill the old pawnbroker, Alyona Ivanova. After he does so, he enjoys hiding the fact, then finally confesses and goes to Siberia. The complication is obvious — Raskolnikov committed what might have been the perfect crime. Even though the police might never have discovered enough evidence for a conviction, he decides to give himself up and to suffer the penalty of the law.

Two factors bring Raskolnikov to the point of confession: his meeting with Marmeladov and his family, and the situation of his sister Dounia. His caring for Marmeladov introduces him to Sonia, who is to become his confessor. The arrival of Dounia and his mother causes the appearance of Svidrigailov, whose sinister nature repulses Raskolnikov. The emergence of Sonia as a full-blown character parallels the development of Raskolnikov's need to tell about his crime. And when he divulges his secret to her, Svidrigailov overhears and acts to use the information for his own end — to attain Dounia. Thus the two external factors come together, and Raskolnikov's confession to the police is a direct consequence of this.

The psychology of the murderer is explored through the cat-and-mouse game played between Raskolnikov and the police, chiefly represented by Porfiry Petrovitch. As in the tales of Edgar Allan Poe, this aspect of the plot pits two very intelligent minds against each other, with every detail of the crime being examined rationally against a background of constant tension between the two powerful personalities. Razumihin serves to confuse and heighten the activity with the police, since he has friends at the police station and communicates with them frequently.

Setting

St. Petersburg, crowded with people, is the main setting, with provincial Russia and the larger world forming a background to this mid-nineteenth-century city. The life of the lower classes, with its squalor and filth, its overcrowding, and its confused or non-existent values, is in contrast to the leisured life of a few gentlemen. The city is so crowded — in the open streets, in the taverns, in the living spaces, in the police station — that the fact that there are no witnesses to Raskolnikov's crime seems almost miraculous. Further, the brutality of existence in the city contrasts with the attempts of the students and intellectuals to rise above their surroundings.

The details of the city's geography are vivid and evoke a distinct sense of what it was like to live in St. Petersburg at the time. But in some respects the city is more than particular locations or details: it becomes a symbol of the world of humanity as a whole, with its limitations and possibilities. In the religious images and allusions to the hundred signs of depravity and sin, the range of human life is surveyed. Privacy in this world is almost impossible, and poverty drives even the most noble of men and women to evil.

The quality of the setting is in part a function of the quality of mind of the major characters who emerge from it. Raskolnikov and Svidrigailov are acute observers of the city's details, and they can interpret the setting in human terms. Seen through their eyes, the river bank or a dwelling or a bridge becomes an almost sacred space, such as the one Raskolnikov describes when he thinks of the meaning of life against the vast allurements of death. In this setting of viciousness and degradation, signs of genuine charity are few, and they do not come out of the framework of traditional Russian Orthodoxy. They often come from people involved in evil.

For Raskolnikov, the choices of setting beyond St. Petersburg are death or Siberia. He chooses to go to Siberia and live, chiefly because he has been able to achieve a link with humanity through Sonia. For Svidrigailov things are otherwise. He chooses self-inflicted death. The landscape he dreams of escaping to (America) is like paradise. But it is unattainable. Svidrigailov cannot make a bridge to humanity through Dounia or anyone else. He chooses self-inflicted death. Clearly, St. Petersburg is the place of ordinary life, while Siberia and America are merely abstractions for the two most powerful male figures.

Character

Dostoevsky is a master of incisive psychological portraiture, but how does he achieve such variety and distinctiveness of character types when he presents so many? Dostoevsky's characters are never simple. In fact, they derive some of their strength from the contradictory elements they embody. Raskolnikov is rational and also nearly mad; Svidrigailov is urbane and cultured, yet depraved and empty at the core. But Dostoevsky's technique goes beyond the use of contradictions.

One technique used is the relating of powerful characters to the central character. Raskolnikov is not only the central figure in the book; his mentality is also a composite of those of the other major characters in the story. Porfiry is rational, like Raskolnikov, and their game of intellectual chess gains from their being well matched in this respect. Svidrigailov and Raskolnikov share the strange idea of the privilege of the criminal class; they consider many of the same options, including suicide, though they draw opposite conclusions. Marmeladov and Raskolnikov share feelings about Sonia, who is their common bond to humanity. Lebeziatnikov and Raskolnikov share freethinking. It is as if Dostoevsky had unpacked Raskolnikov's psychology aspect by aspect and created separate characters from each aspect found. The likenesses are great enough for differences to be particularly noticeable.

Dostoevsky's characters are not only reflective of Raskolnikov; they are reflective of each other too. The hero himself sees likenesses in the actions of Sonia and Dounia, and compares himself to Svidrigailov. Pulcheria distinguishes her daughter's two suitors only after drawing their similarities first. Katerina Ivanovna and Pulcheria Raskolnikov are opposites. By creating characters who explicitly or implicitly are meant to be compared and/or contrasted, Dostoevsky both highlights individual traits and implies a larger continuity. A common thread of humanity is visible in the fabric of the whole community, each character being related to some other within the design. Can you suggest other parallels and contrasts?

Theme

A theme can sometimes be summed up in a word, like *suicide*, *despair*, *suffering*, *life*, *money*, etc. More important than the choice of theme in a literary work is the way the theme is developed. In this novel the theme of suffering is given profound development. Sonia is a focus for this theme, for she serves as an absorber of suffering — her own and that of others. The torture of life itself induces suffering in the Marmeladov family in particular. Where Marmeladov is paralyzed by it, his wife Katerina is driven mad. Suffering is caused by evil, yet it is a remedy for the guilt that can be produced by commission of a crime. Raskolnikov chooses suffering over death, and Siberia is the landscape in which suffering can be channelled into redemption.

The title of the novel combines two major themes — crime and punishment — which are embodied in the murders, and the confession and sentencing. But unlike the detective type of novel, (which was then in its infancy), this novel has themes that go beyond crime. Guilt, the family, individuality, and alienation are a few of the themes that give depth to the novel. In fact it can be argued that societal themes (i.e., the theme of religion) are wholly inadequate to explain the power of the novel. Although the novel seems to be about crime, in the sense that there is a progression from the freethinking of Raskolnikov's article on the permissibility of crime to the traditional notion that crime must not pay, actually Raskolnikov progresses from a disregard for the value of human life to an affirmation of it, in his growing relationship with Sonia.

The theme of money is complex. Both excess money and lack of money cause problems. Poverty is in part the cause of Raskolnikov's murder of the old pawnbroker and is wholly the cause of Sonia's prostitution. Svidrigailov is not made good by his possession of wealth, even though he does perform a few good deeds, such as helping the Marmeladov children. Poverty among the intelligentsia, particularly students, is acute, but its greatest pinch is felt by people like Marmeladov, whose problem is lack of will. Money for Marmeladov means drinking and forgetting his responsibility, but money does not change his basic drive toward escape. Raskolnikov has almost as little regard for money as Marmeladov. He depends on others to provide money for him, and he spends it with abandon once he has it. Of course, he does not spend it on drink, but gives it away with apparent liberality. Although he bridles at his sister's having to consider money in her marriage plans, he offers no alternative. Clearly the economic situation in St. Petersburg at the time of the novel was difficult, but Dostoevsky uses poverty as a test of character.

More complex than money is the theme of religion. Characters who bring out this theme are Lizaveta Ivanovna, Sonia, and through Sonia, Raskolnikov. One character passes the torch to the other. By a strange progression, Raskolnikov comes to the Bible through the person he has killed to perfect his crime — Lizaveta. Yet the problem of religion is not simple. Alyona Ivanovna, the pawnbroker, is surrounded by religious paraphernalia in her room, but she is not portrayed as religious. And Raskolnikov does not become religious in any ordinary sense through his ordeal. He shows interest in biblical stories, in the cypress-wood cross and the New Testament, but his decision-making is based more on psychology than on Christianity. His atonement is that demanded by the law, not by the Word. One of the great ironies of the book is the association of two sinners — Raskolnikov and Svidrigailov — with the Bible. However Russian Orthodoxy, as a doctrine, is not a dominant theme, and Christianity is used superficially, more as a sign of a human bond between Sonia and Raskolnikov than a clear indication of a conversion experience. Though Dostoevsky was a product of a Christian culture, he shared the new concern with fundamentally human and psychological relationships.

Symbolism

A symbol is an object or other sensory impression with power and meaning beyond its face value. Dostoevsky uses traditional symbols as well as those evolved in his own imagination. One traditional symbol, the Christian cross, is given by Sonia to Raskolnikov, but it is more representative of the bond between them than of Raskolnikov's new faith in Jesus. Another traditional symbol — the wheel of fortune — is used in the death of Marmeladov. The unfortunate man is crushed repeatedly under a revolving carriage wheel, just as life itself has cast him down again and again. Here the traditional symbol is buried within the context.

Two symbols with seemingly opposite meanings are fresh air, which Porfiry says Raskolnikov needs, and the restrictive patch of space that represents life itself to Raskolnikov. The fresh air represents atonement and a new perspective, which will, in Porfiry's opinion, open Raskolnikov to the fullness of life. The image of a small square of space represents, in Raskolnikov's mind, the joy of living when he is in the throes of guilt. Even within the crowded atmosphere of St. Petersburg, Raskolnikov can relish life's promise.

There is also symbolism in the green shawl that Sonia wears. Green is the traditional color of hope, and her actions give hope to her destitute family. In addition, the green shawl signifies life itself, for Sonia gives Raskolnikov a second chance at life. The green is especially striking since, except for the red blood of Raskolnikov's victims, very little color is used in the book.

The symbolic use of *landscape* is explored in the section above on setting; the symbolic use of *character* is alluded to in the section above on character. In short, Dostoevsky mixes symbols and mundane details, achieving a picture of a world in which not everything presented is fraught with meaning, but there is enough to suggest the larger dimensions of the story being presented.

Allusion

The novel is richly allusive, as might be expected of a work about intellectuals in a university town. The most important allusions are the most obvious. For example, the allusion to Lazarus is underscored by a quotation of the whole story from Scripture. Lazarus is mentioned more than once, and Raskolnikov takes a special interest in him. The biblical message is clear — Jesus brought the dead man back to life. But there is not a direct parallel between Raskolnikov and Lazarus, for who then would be the parallel for Jesus? Certainly not Porfiry! Raskolnikov relates his situation to that of Lazarus in some unspecified way. He feels a need to emerge from one state to another and to have a sense of renewal. (The fact that he hears the story of Lazarus read by Sonia from a Bible given to her by Lizaveta Ivanovna is ironical to the reader, though not the hero.) In a sense, Raskolnikov's passage from pure intellectuality to the full enjoyment and appreciation of human values, is the progress of a Lazarus, as Dostoevsky implies in the final image of Raskolnikov reaching under his pillow for his Bible.

The range of allusions is broad, covering many European literatures, as well as popular culture. Raskolnikov alludes to Jack the Giant-killer and to Punch and Judy. Svidrigailov makes allusions to classical literature. Allusions are used ironically by Marmeladov, whose constant use of themes from Revelation signals his later suicide. Allusions are used meaningfully by Porfiry, who probes Raskolnikov's psyche through what he understands best — his learning.

Dream Visions and Psychology

Two key dream visions, opposite in effect, are used at opposite ends of the novel. The first one, Raskolnikov's dream about Mikolka and the mare, projects the kind of mindless brutality Raskolnikov himself is about to engage in, and in some way the dream permits him to follow through with his plan. Raskolnikov becomes a kind of Mikolka, while Alyona Ivanovna has the role of Mikolka's mare. This dream precedes and foreshadows the act.

The other dream is the one Svidrigailov has about the five-year-old girl who is apparently innocent but actually lascivious. Her image triggers his suicide. In a sense this vision summarizes Svidrigailov's outlook on life. Sophistication and depravity are everywhere. Like the rats that seem to infest his last lodging, ideas of sensual degradation haunt him to the end.

Raskolnikov dreams about real innocence and the horror of mechanical brutality, but he ultimately moves to an acceptance of a fundamental humanity. Svidrigailov, however, dreams about the impossibility of innocence or humanity; he might well have ravished the child if she had been real, not just a dream.

Dostoevsky seems to have anticipated the present-day research of Ira Progoff into the power of dreams and images to release men to act. Action seems to be an inevitable consequence of both the above dreams — action that is destructive, mechanical, pre-planned. Raskolnikov's is anticipated not only by rehearsals but by exhaustive planning of every detail of the execution. He acts according to a method rather than an impulse, from the article he writes down to the care with which he prepares to carry the axe. From the broad theory to the details of execution the act is laid out. Events conspire with him to provide an opportunity. And he is psychologically purged by the dream about Mikolka.

Svidrigailov's action seems more impulsive than Raskolnikov's; nevertheless, it is mechanical and seems rehearsed, or at least carefully stage-managed, like all of his other actions. In a way he "atones" before he commits suicide, by providing for Marmeladov's three orphaned children. Where Raskolnikov moves from theory to reality, Svidrigailov moves from reality to theory. Even his desire to go to America, the new land of innocence (so he thinks), is only wishful thinking. Unable to change himself, and seeing both himself and the world embroiled in corruption, Svidrigailov makes the final exit.

Psychologically, this suicide allows the reader to participate in the "fresh air" of Raskolnikov's atonement — the symbol of corruption has been eliminated.

Point of View

Dostoevsky's novel is written in the third person, from an objective point of view. Because the narrator is omniscient and knows the characters' thoughts, the psychological reactions become part of the objective presentation. Raskolnikov's thoughts as well as the details of the murders are given. His horror during the act and his fears of being apprehended push him to the brink of sanity. We not only witness what he sees, but also what he thinks. Thus he becomes a real human being for the reader.

In a similar manner, Svidrigailov is humanized through the exposure of his thoughts. At first, he appears only as a menacing figure in Pulcheria's letter. Then gradually, through reports of his atrocities, he grows into a personification of evil. Finally he appears, and his actions are measured against his less-forbidding self. When the narrator opens up Svidrigailov's mind late in the book, the character becomes almost pathetic, though much of the mystery of his evil is left to die with him.

Because there is more than one criminal intellect in the novel, Dostoevsky is able to develop aspects of this intellect that go beyond that which one character might reveal. Raskolnikov and Svidrigailov are seen as "doubles" in large degree so that they can be differentiated in the end.

We can learn as much about Dostoevsky's point of view by cataloging the characters whose thoughts we are *never* allowed to read, as by examining those we are. For example, although the external reactions of Porfiry are noted, the intricate workings of his mind are left a dark secret. This is why his treatment of Raskolnikov seems remarkable. He seems to work toward the young man's betterment, yet he achieves his aim by arguing against himself. The interchange between investigator and criminal before the final confession is a masterpiece of reverse psychology, as well as an argument for the value of life. This is not to say that great sinister motives are at work behind Porfiry's apparent humanity. Rather, the functioning of a mind not at the frontier of man's experience held little interest for the author.

By fully exploring the minds of criminal figures, and not others, Dostoevsky fulfilled the promise of his title.

Selected Criticisms

Crime and Punishment was Fyodor Dostoevski's first popularly successful novel after his nine-year imprisonment and exile for alleged political crimes (the charges were of doubtful validity) against the czar. After his release from penal servitude, Dostoevski published novels, short stories, novelettes, and journalistic pieces, but none of these brought him the critical and popular acclaim which in 1866 greeted Crime and Punishment—possibly his most popular novel. This book is no simple precursor of the detective novel, no simplistic mystery story to challenge the minds of Russian counterparts to Sherlock Holmes' fans. It is a complex story of a man's turbulent inner life and his relationship to others and to society at large. The book must be considered within the matrix of Dostoevski's convictions at the time he wrote the novel, because Dostoevski's experience with czarist power made a lasting impression on his thinking. Indeed, Dostoevski himself made such an evaluation possible by keeping detailed notebooks on the development of his novels and on his problems with fleshing out plots and characters.

Chastened by his imprisonment and exile, Dostoevski shifted his position from the youthful liberalism (certainly not radicalism), which seemed to have precipitated his incarceration, to a mature conservatism which embraced many, perhaps most, of the traditional views of his time. Thus Dostoevski came to believe that legal punishment was not a deterrent to crime because he was convinced that criminals demanded to be punished; that is, they had a spiritual need to be punished. Today, we might call that compulsion masochistic. But Dostoevski, in his time, related the tendency to mystical concepts of the Eastern Orthodox Church, an Establishment institution. With a skeptical hostility toward Western religion and culture, born of several years of living abroad, Dostoevski became convinced that the Western soul was bankrupt and that salvation—one of his major preoccupations—was possible only under the influence of the Church and an ineffable love for Mother Russia, a devotion to homeland, to the native soil, which would brook neither logic nor common sense: a dedication beyond reason or analysis. Thus, expiation for sins was attained through atonement, a rite of purification.

However, the required expiation is complicated in Crime and Punishment by the split personality—a typically Dostoevskian ploy—of the protagonist. The schizophrenia of Raskolnikov is best illustrated by his ambivalent motives for murdering the pawnbroker. At first, Raskolnikov views his heinous crime as an altruistic act which puts the pawnbroker and her sister out of their misery while providing him the necessary financial support to further his education and mitigate his family's poverty, thus relieving unbearable pressures on him. And he intends to atone for his misdeeds by subsequently living an upright life dedicated to humanitarian enterprises. But Raskolnikov shortly becomes convinced of his own superiority. Indeed, he divides the human race into "losers" and "winners": the former, meek and submissive; the latter, Nietzschean supermen who can violate any law or principle to attain their legitimately innovative and presumably beneficial ends. And Raskolnikov allies himself with the "superman" faction. He intends to prove his superiority by committing murder and justifying it on the basis of his own superiority. This psychological configuration is common enough, but, unlike most paranoid schizophrenics, Raskolnikov carries his design through—a signal tribute to the depth of his convictions.

The results are predictably confusing. The reader is as puzzled about Raskolnikov's motives as he is. Is it justifiable to commit an atrocity in the name of improvement of the human condition? This essential question remains unanswered in *Crime and Punishment* because Raskolnikov, egocentrically impelled by pride, cannot decide whether or not he is superior, one of those supermen entitled to violate any law of any principle to serve the cause of ultimate justice, however justice might be construed. Likewise, in his notebooks, Dostoevski implied that he, too, was ambivalent about Raskolnikov's motives. Yet he added that he was not a psychologist but a novelist who plumbed the depths of men's souls; in other words, he had a religious not a secular orientation. He was thus more concerned with consequences than with causality. This carefully planned novel therefore expands upon a philosophical problem embodied in the protagonist.

The philosophical problem in *Crime and Punishment* constitutes the central theme of the novel: the lesson Raskolnikov has to learn, the precept he has to master in order to redeem himself. The protagonist finally has to concede that free will is limited. He has to discover and admit that he cannot control and direct his life solely with his reason and intellect, as he tried to do, for such a plan leads only to emptiness and to sinful intellectual pride. Abstract reason takes the place of a fully-lived life and precludes the happiness of a fully-lived life; happiness must be earned, and it can be earned only through suffering. Thus Raskolnikov has to learn that happiness is achieved through suffering—another typically Dostoevskian mystical concept. Hence, the climactic moment in the novel comes when Raskolnikov confesses his guilt at the police station, for Raskolnikov's confession is tantamount to a request for punishment for the crime and acceptance of his need to suffer. In this way, Raskolnikov demonstrates the basic message of *Crime and Punishment:* that reason does not bring happiness; happiness is earned through suffering.

The Epilogue—summarizing the fates of the other characters;

78

Raskolnikov's trial, his sentencing, and his prison term; and Sonia's devotion to Raskolnikov during his imprisonment—confirms the novel's central theme. Artistically, however, the Epilogue is somewhat less than satisfactory or satisfying. First of all, Dostoevski's notes indicate that he had considered and rejected an alternate ending in which Raskolnikov committed suicide. Such a conclusion would have been logical in an existential sense. And it would have been psychologically sound. However, the very logicality of Raskolnikov's suicide would have suggested a triumph of reason over the soul. That idea was not consonant with Dostoevski's convictions; thus, he dropped the plan. Second, the ending which Dostoevski finally wrote in the Epilogue implies that the meek and submissive side of Raskolnikov's personality emerged completely victorious over the superman. But such an ending contradicts Raskolnikov's persistent duality throughout the novel. Raskolnikov's dramatic conversion thus strains credulity, for it seems too pat a resolution of the plot. For the sophisticated reader, however, it does not greatly detract from the powerful psychological impact of the novel proper nor diminish the quality of a genuinely serious attempt to confront simultaneously a crucial social problem and a deeply profound individual, human one.

Joanne G. Kashdan

. . . . The details fill two volumes . . . . in all of which there is not one dull line. The power of the book lies in its marvelous dissection of intricate mental characteristics—in its unaffected intensity of realism—in a verisimilitude so extraordinary that the reader is compelled to believe himself the criminal, to feel the fascination of the crime, to endure the excitement of it, to enjoy the perpetration of it, to vibrate with the terror of it, to suffer all the nightmares, all the horrors, all the degradation, all the punishment of it. That is what causes so terrible a nervous strain upon the reader. He *actually* becomes Raskolnikoff the murderer, and feels, thinks, dreams, trembles as the criminal whose psychology is thus exposed for him! The perusal of the pages seems to produce a sort of avatar, a change of souls; if the reader is not wholly Raskolnikoff, he is at least wholly Dostoievsky the author, nearly crazed by his own thoughts. And all the personages of the narrative live with the same violence of realism . . . .

Lafcadio Hearn

Raskolnikov is a noble soul corrupted by a false philosophy. He has committed murder and theft, but there is nothing mean or sensual about him. Svidrigailov is, on the side of sensuality, what Raskolnikov is on the side of pride . . . the main purpose that he serves in developing the theme is to present to Raskolnikov a picture of what his theories might involve in a person whose weakness is for women.

Raskolnikov abhors Svidrigailov; he thinks him the vilest of the vile. But Svidrigailov knows that Raskolnikov is a murderer, and has therefore a certain moral advantage over him. And he seems always to be in his path. It is not an agreeable situation for Raskolnikov. It is as if another self, a viler self, were perpetually there to remind him how vile he is.

The best of it is that Svidrigailov is a complete and independent character, with his own history and his own way of solving his problem—in his case . . . it is by suicide. And, moreover, it is not Dostoevski who tells us that he has this kind of symbolical relation to Raskolnikov. We draw that conclusion without the least prompting by the author. So that if Svidrigailov is an important factor in driving Raskolnikov to confession and expiation, this is but another reminder of how completely the philosophical theme is in this novel dramatized in the story.

Joseph Warren Beach

Men of real genius, authentic benefactors of mankind, do not look on themselves as supermen for whom all things are lawful; on the contrary, they do great things for the world by sacrificing themselves to that which they put above man. Raskolnikov was a divided being, from whom freedom was already alienated by his inner unhealthiness, whereas the truly great are integral and jealous for their own unity. Dostoevsky showed the folly of claiming to be a superman, a lying idea that is the death of man: this claim and all its cognate aspirations sooner or later collapse into a state of pitiable weakness and futility which is no longer human, and against it the true nature of religious and moral consciousness stands out with everlasting majesty. The sin and the powerlessness of man in his pretension to almightiness are revealed in sorrow and anguish; the tortured conscience of Raskolnikov is a witness not only to his transgression but also to his weakness.

Nicholas Berdyaev

We must not ignore the weaknesses and the contradictions of Dostoyevsky. But what matters, in the final reckoning, is the wealth of his visions. Fyodor Dostoyevsky is one great novelist who has been able to strike off fiery lyrics out of the agonized chaos of existence. The riddle of life—with which all genuine literature, and Russian literature especially, is saturated—has through his pen become transmuted and ennobled. He has gone down to the darkest places, into the obscurest nooks of mind and matter, of impulse and urge, of vice and sublimity, and out of it all he has woven a passionate symphony, hard and irregular, rising to heights of intense terror and tenderness. Dostoyevsky is often crude, melodramatic, lurid, but never cold, and always the supreme psychologist, the prober of the obscure, the impassioned analyst of revolting forces that "normal" people are pleased to call "pathological."

N. Bryllion Fagin

Having ridiculed the concept of the rationally virtuous revolutionary hero, and every premise on which he stood, Dostoevsky set about in *Crime and Punishment* . . . to convert him. Raskolnikov is the first Dostoevskyan version of the revolutionary "new man," the proud, active Western-oriented rationalist who imagines that he is independent of all codes of morality. Raskolnikov acts decisively—by committing two murders—and his act is shown to have symbolic meaning in many spheres of human activity and belief. It is then Dostoevsky's intention to strip away successive layers of rationalization and show that in all spheres this kind of "reasoned" act is evil and insane. Raskolnikov's controversial conversion in Siberia to Sonya's ethic of submissive and limitless love for mankind, although it strains credibility to the limit, is meant to conclude his journey from evil to good, from a rebellious individualism in which "all is permitted," to a pious acquiescence in the way things are, however painful and unjust.

Rufus W. Mathewson

If we consider the beginning and end of *Crime and Punishment,* we find that Raskolnikov goes from pride to humility, hate to love, reason to faith, and from separation from his fellow men to communion with them. The emotions, attitudes, and values at the beginning balance antithetically with those at the end. In the most general sense, then, the structure of the novel is built on a change from the hero's belief in one set of values to a set opposite in character . . . .

. . . In the last pages before the epilogue, Raskolnikov takes up the cross Sonia offers him "without knowing why," and in his inability to speak out the words of confession on Hay Market Square, Dostoevsky "shows" us in one small scene how difficult it will be for Raskolnikov to humble himself before what his nature has dictated and his own essential being has chosen. The novel should end there. If Dostoevsky wished to represent Raskolnikov's battle against conscious acquiescence to the dictates of his unconscious nature—all of which he summarizes for us in the epilogue—he should have written another volume. The epilogue follows logically, but not artistically.

Edward Wasiolek

He [Dostoevsky] distinguishes primarily between those who assert themselves selfishly, even viciously—the "dark souls"—and those who use their free will in the way God desires them to use it—by subordinating their will to the divine. These are the "bearers of light." To assert oneself is to destroy oneself; the way of salvation lies only in a voluntary surrender of oneself to God. This essentially Christian insight affords us an understanding of Dostoevsky's deep-seated conviction that human moral freedom, being generally wrongly used, is a fearful responsibility and a tragic aspect of human nature. Its chronic abuse is the cause of man's misery and the source of humankind's woes and evils. This is the Fall of man—his self-centeredness, self-assertion (what Nietzsche called the Will-to-Power) and what Christian theology has always designated as the original sin. It results in suffering and terrible evils, both individual and social. And the tragic thing about it is that it is self-caused: man has chosen evil of his own volition, not because of some impersonal fate or environmental conditions—certainly not because of God's fiat!

Matthew Spinka

The word "suffering" . . . in Dostoevsky's novels has a wider meaning than man's usual ordeals. According to his view, suffering is twofold. First, man suffers involuntarily because he is not able to gratify his desires or attain his ideal, if his aspirations are impeded or his potentialities suppressed. He suffers, further, in his rebellion against mental agony, when he violently refuses to accept his fate. In his attempts to free himself from spiritual pain, man often applies means which bring suffering not only to himself but to the people around him. Second, there occurs in Dostoevsky's novels a type of suffering without rebellion. Submitting completely to their destiny, Dostoevsky's passive characters make no attempt to evade their ordeals, but accept them as ordained and justified by God. In consequence they live only for others, specifically for the purpose of loving others. Therefore, the notion of suffering becomes intimately connected with the concept of love.

Temira Pachmuss

At no point . . . does Dostoevsky permit his protagonist consciously to recognize his error, consciously to arrive at a new level of awareness. Raskolnikov does not achieve an insight into his condition as do Macbeth and Lear. He answers, rather, Henry James's requirement that the protagonist must not be "too priggishly, too divinely clever." Governing the formidable obstacles imposed by the dominating point of view from which the novel is conducted—Dostoevsky proves his sovereign command of his fluid, ambiguous "center" by forbidding the protagonist's consciousness to assimilate a vast body of data eloquently meaningful to the illumination of his being. The data which glide over the consciousness of Raskolnikov, must be gathered, assimilated, retained, and measured against his movement by the reader, who alone is to achieve the insight denied the protagonist. It is among other things the difficulty of this task which makes the reading of the novel the memorable and rewarding experience that it is.

Pearl C. Niemi

Crime and Punishment is not only the first of Dostoevsky's stories in which religion plays any part, it is the first in which the double's dilemma is worked out in terms of inwardness. It is also the only novel in which a double is purged. Is Raskolnikov really a double, and does he exhibit affective and moral ambivalence? . . . Raskolnikov does indeed wobble back and forth between the claims of pride and pity. . . . he understands that the interior battle *is* essentially between reason as an instrument of the ego's desire for power and glory, and the heart's sorrow for others. . . . He represses pity as long as it gets in the way of the egoism that his rational crime is fed by. But he never denies the necessity of pity. "Pain and suffering are always inevitable for a large intelligence and a deep heart. The really great men must, I think, have great sadness on earth." Not only does he never deny pity, he is constantly tortured by his Titanic pride. He has an instinct within him that solemnly condemns him even while he refuses to listen. In Raskolnikov too the contradictions exist side by side. Repression only acts to elevate one side, it does not make the other any less active. Time after time Raskolnikov's pity produces works of compassion, charity, and self-sacrifice. What makes his simultaneity or doubleness look different is that his reason remains active on one level, and pity on another. . . . *Crime and Punishment* is the story of the half-conscious debate of inwardness rising slowly and surely to a fully conscious plane. Raskolnikov confesses to the police, not because he has failed or been caught, but because he knows he cannot resolve the torment of this questionableness or suppress the inward debate.

Ralph Harper

Suggested Study Topics

1. *Crime and Punishment* has been read as a murder-mystery and detective story. How do you view it?

2. Dostoevsky wrote, "They call me a psychologist. It is not true. I am only a realist in the higher sense; that is, I portray all the depths of the human soul." Do you consider *Crime and Punishment* to be a psychological novel?

3. Do you agree with those critics who feel that the epilogue is "weak," or those who maintain that the epilogue "ruined" the novel?

4. In his notebooks for the novel, Dostoevsky has Raskolnikov shoot himself. Do you think that Raskolnikov's suicide would have made for a more effective ending?

5. What is Raskolnikov's punishment? Do you feel that the punishment fits the crime?

6. What concepts of law are prominent in *Crime and Punishment*?

7. How do dreams function in the novel?

8. What does Dostoevsky gain artistically by representing Sonia as a prostitute? What biblical character did he likely have in mind?

9. Choose the incidents which seem to be major crises in Raskolnikov's life and determine what each contributes to his development.

10. Examine carefully the scene in which Sonia reads to Raskolnikov the story of Lazarus. How does Raskolnikov's condition resemble that of Lazarus?

11. What irony and value are there in making Sonia the principal outside agent of Raskolnikov's redemption?

12. What is the relationship of Raskolnikov's confession to Sonia and his confession at the police station?

13. The structure of the novel allows Raskolnikov to have alternate interviews with Sonia and Svidrigailov. How does this structure reflect thematic development?

14. Enumerate and record the different reasons given by Raskolnikov for his crime, after he has committed it. Add those given by Luzhin, Porfiry, Svidrigailov and Sonia. Does any reliable conclusion emerge?

15. What is the purpose of the second murder? If it had not happened we would never notice the difference. Why does Raskolnikov never consider Lizaveta in his explanations? Does her death merely add a kind of irresistible, mechanical "realism" to the book, or has it some other significance?

Bibliography

Beach, Joseph Warren. *The Twentieth Century Novel: Studies in Technique.* New York: Appleton-Century-Crofts, 1932.

Berdyaev, Nicholas. *Dostoevsky.* New York: Sheed & Ward, 1934; Cleveland; Meridian Books, World Publishing Company, 1957.

Carr, Edward Hallett. *Dostoevsky (1821-1881).* New York: Houghton, Mifflin Company, 1931; New York: Barnes & Noble, 1962.

De Jonge, Alex. *Dostoevsky & the Age of Intensity.* New York: St. Martin's, 1975.

Dostoevsky, Fyodor. *The Notebooks for Crime and Punishment.* Edited and translated by Edward Wasiolek. Chicago: The University of Chicago Press, 1967.

Fanger, Donald. *Dostoevsky and Romantic Realism.* Cambridge, Massachusetts: Harvard University Press, 1965.

Frank, Joseph. *Dostoevsky: The Seeds of Revolt, 1821-1849.* Princeton: Princeton University Press, 1976.

Fueloep-Miller, René. *Fyodor Dostoevsky: Insight, Faith and Prophecy.* New York: Charles Scribner's Sons, 1950.

Gibian, George (ed.) *Crime and Punishment.* (The Coulson Translation; Backgrounds and Sources; Essays in Criticism.) New York: W. W. Norton & Company, 1964.

Gide, André. *Dostoevsky.* New York: Alfred A. Knopf, 1926; New York: New Directions, 1961.

Hingley, Ronald. *The Undiscovered Dostoyevsky.* London: Hamish Hamilton, 1962.

Ivanov, Vyacheslav. *Freedom and the Tragic Life: A Study in Dostoevsky.* New York: Noonday Press, 1957.

Magarshack, David. *Dostoevsky.* New York: Harcourt, Brace & World, 1963.

Mirsky, Dmitri S. *A History of Russian Literature.* Edited by Francis J. Whitfield, New York: Alfred A. Knopf, 1960.

Modern Fiction Studies. Vol. IV, No. 3 (Autumn, 1958). Dostoevsky Number. Critical studies and selected checklist of criticisms and translations. (Note: each Winter Number contains an index.)

Muchnic, Helen. *An Introduction to Russian Literature.* New York: E. P. Dutton & Company, 1964.

Pachmuss, Temira. *F. M. Dostoevsky: Dualism and Synthesis of the Human Soul.* Carbondale, Illinois: Southern Illinois University Press, 1963.

Reeve, F. D. *The Russian Novel.* New York: McGraw-Hill Book Company, 1966.

Seduro, Vladimir. *Dostoyevski in Russian Literary Criticism, 1846-1956.* New York: Columbia University Press, 1957.

Simmons, Ernest J. *Dostoevsky: The Making of a Novelist.* New York: Oxford University Press, 1940; New York: Vintage Books, Random House, 1962.

Simmons, Ernest J. *Introduction to Russian Realism.* Bloomington, Indiana: Indiana University Press, 1965.

Slonim, Marc. *The Epic of Russian Literature: From Its Origins through Tolstoy.* New York: Oxford University Press, 1950.

Spinka, Matthew. *Christian Thought from Erasmus to Berdyaev.* Englewood Cliffs, New Jersey: Prentice-Hall, Inc., 1962.

Wasiolek, Edward (ed.) *Crime and Punishment and the Critics.* Belmont, California: Wadsworth Publishing Company, 1961.

Wasiolek, Edward. *Dostoevsky: The Major Fiction.* Cambridge, Massachusetts: The M.I.T. Press, 1964.

Wellek, René (ed.) *Dostoevsky: A Collection of Critical Essays.* Englewood Cliffs, New Jersey: Prentice-Hall, Inc., 1962.

Yarmolinsky, Avrahm. *Dostoevsky: His Life and Art.* New York: Criterion Books, 1957; New York: Evergreen Books, Grove Press, 1960.

NOTES

NOTES